Just Her Poetry

Just Her Poetry

Seasons of a Soul

D.L. Finn

Just Her Poetry: Seasons of a Soul
Copyright © 2019 D.L. Finn
All rights reserved.

No part of this book may be reproduced in any written, electronic, recording, or photocopying without written permission of the publisher or author. The exception would be in the case of brief quotations embodied in the critical articles or reviews and pages where permission is specifically granted by the publisher or author.

Cover by: Monica Gibson
monicagibson.com

Photographs: D.L. Finn

Book design by: Maureen Cutajar
gopublished.com

This is a work of fiction. The names, characters, places, or events used in this book are the product of the author's imagination or used fictitiously. Any resemblance to actual people, alive or deceased, events or locales is completely coincidental.

ISBN Print: 978-0-9977519-9-4
ISBN eBook: 978-0-9977519-8-7

Library of Congress number: 2019901902

D.C. Hawk Publishing

D.L. Finn
www.dlfinnauthor.com

Contents

NATURE: *Spring and Summer* 1
NATURE: *Fall and Winter* 69
MUSING FROM THE BACK OF A HARLEY 97
THE EMOTIONS: *Darkness and Light* 129
THE EMOTIONS: *Those Feelings* 175
FROM THE BOOK WORLD 189
A BIT OF FAMILY 201
HOLIDAYS AND VACATIONS 209
BONUS POETRY 229
SOME READERS' FAVORITES: *No Fairy Tale* 235
AUTHOR'S NOTE 248
ABOUT THE AUTHOR 249

Just Her Poetry

NATURE
Spring and Summer

THE GATHERING

At my feet they gather in peace...
As the sun reflects off their fur.
They quickly find their sunny spot...
Ears alert as bird songs fill the air.
A bee examines our assemblage...
Its presence startles a relaxing cat.
Our gathering expands deeply...
Into the blooming fertile landscape.
The gentle breeze...
Blows away the remnants of winter.
The blue skies showcase the beauty...
In an abstract painting of an untamed scene.
A woodpecker in the distant tree...
Is loudly searching for the awakening insects.
Yes, the long winter nap is over...
And we gather in the moment to rejoice together.

SPRING SUN

I sit outside in the spring sun
Listening to the birds sing
As a bee hums near me searching.
Small patches of snow are slushy
Everything's waking up from the dormant season
The cats are exploring...the dogs sunbathing.
I relax in the warmth that renews my soul.
It is a day for new beginnings...a new seed
A place to plant buried dreams in the stars
In the fertile magic of a perfect day in spring.

SIT ALONE

I sit alone on our deck
Blanketed in the sun's warm rays,
The bird's chirps and trills
Fill the silent space.

Our big black cat
Looks for his prey,
And chases away the bees
Who wander into my presence.

Our dogs lazy on their backs
In the backyard with their paws in the air,
Like a yoga pose
Welcoming the warmth.

Distant pond frogs sing their loud chorus
A lone cloud floats by,
Reminding me of the winter past
And storms yet to come.

But right now it is time to bask
In what spring has brought,
So, for this moment
I sit blissfully alone.

PLANT

Today is the first warm day of spring
I step outside excited to sit in the sun
The bare trees are starting to bud
Green pine needles reach for the clear blue sky.
Birds are singing, while gathering for their nests
The bees find daffodils and lilies to satisfy their hunger
The bear has awakened from its winter nap,
Tipping over its first full garbage can.
Pine cones scattered amongst those littered from fall
The air heavy with rebirth, it's time to plant my seeds
Not just introducing them to the soil, but in my mind
To grow and thrive like the magical landscape around me
Nurtured in love and hope for another season of growth
When mistakes and lessons are the fertile base
As I reach for the stars with my dreams
Spring reminds me that all is possible if you just plant it.

REMOVE

I remove the blue hat and two branches from the wooden
　chair.
Setting them aside, I wonder when I'll use them again
Since the snowperson that held them has melted away
Along with the bitter cold of the season.
The birds have returned in song building their nests.
I sit in a deck chair absorbing the day into my soul
I'm in a place of magic where all is possible.
Life springing to existence after lying dormant.
It renews, reproduces, and releases its essence
Yet the past season will return
And all will be silent for that time of rest.
But now the spring days in our lives return
And for this moment, I'm embracing them.

RIVER'S JOURNEY

I sit high above the river—observing.
Its twists and turns propel it forward.
The water crashes down the rocky ledges
Leaving spectacular waterfalls to admire.
It's heading for a manmade lake
Where someday it will be released into a river again,
Then its journey continues until it reaches the sea.

It's a long journey ahead for this river.
But, it's also a beautiful reminder
No matter what life throws at me
No matter what obstacles, it keeps flowing forward.
And if I ever find myself stuck in an unmoving lake…
I'll wait until that moment when it is my time of release
Then I can continue my journey to the sea of dreams.

A DAY AT THE RIVER

I woke up feeling alive with the sounds of spring outside my window.
The birds singing, insects humming, and wild creatures abounding.
Chores are forgotten when a day at the river is suggested…
We eagerly pile into the car and arrive at the crowded destination.
Paying to park, we hurry to our favorite pathway of people.
A Harley rumbles by as we reach the start of the experience…
A breathless climb up the hill, we are high above the river.
Surrounded by a green landscape bursting with color
The trees are blooming with pink and white buds.
Flowers abound in orange, white, red, purple, and white.
I do not need to read the "Do Not Pick" sign…I wouldn't.
Instead, with my camera out, I begin to capture the beauty.
Butterflies saturated in beauty fill the air in their nectar quest
Lost in the splendor my husband watches my path…
He's saved me before from stepping on a sunning rattlesnake.
We pause at a favorite bench to record this day into our souls
Soon hand-in-hand we cross a wooden bridge…
Stopping to admire the rocky waterfall's fluid magnificence.
Each person passed is full of smiles that we return
Continuing ahead until we stop at "our" spot
We find a rock by the creek and rehydrate in nature's wonder
Resting in a perfect moment is a gift-given only on a day at the river.

THE DOVE

Spring has arrived
The blue jays are creating their nests
The sun is warming the landscape
The hibernating bears are awakening
Trees are heavy with growth
Flowers are pushing through the soil.
All announcing spring's return...
But, it's the gentle coo of a gray dove
Off in the distance...
That makes it real for me.
I smile...
Silently I welcome the dove back—and spring.

SUN

The sun fills my soul with its warmth
The gentle breeze cools my skin
The windchimes sway in a musical spectacle
The chainsaw roars as it cleans up the past season
The birds warble in distant trees.
These spring sounds soothe my mind
As green bursts through the glory of winter
Everything alive and renewing
It is a peacefully busy time
And my body absorbs this perfection under the sun.

SIT

I sit on a bench in our front yard absorbing the day
The cars race by on the road off in the distance...
But I'm surrounded by nature and the trees.

I hear a branch crackle off to my right
I observe three deer...
They go on eating and ignoring my presence.

Until the mother's brown eyes acknowledge me,
And her nervous does rush to her...
Their ears tall as they pause to watch me.

Satisfied I mean them no harm
They go back to eating unimpressed I am there...
Then my dogs begin whining at our front door.

They're alerting me of these gentle intruders
This scatters the babies as they move to safety...
While the mother carefully follows behind.

My tiger-striped huntress cat watches next to me
Her tail twitching...
Soon the moment is gone as the family of deer move on.

My tiger kitty goes back to cleaning herself, the dogs are quiet
I smile at my encounter with nature...
Sitting on a bench out front, on a beautiful spring day.

MORE

The sun bears down on me in my chair
I move from the deck to the bench in the shade,
Ready to write surrounded by oaks, cedars, dogwoods,
And my quick-growing redwood—a Mother's Day gift.
I note my coming chores now that winter has passed...later
Now, I take in a long deep breath and my shoulders relax.
Our tiger kitty joins me in my moment
I hear a sound and glance over:
A family of deer are calmly grazing a few feet away.
They seem unconcerned with our presence.
The mother moves closer, as her babies slowly follow.

In my most welcoming way I meet the mom's brown eyes.
It lasts for a brief moment but also continues into eternity.
I gently smile—I mean them no harm
The dogs, though, make their existence known.
Babies hop to safety while mom walks into stillness.
I'm grateful for the sun and my moment,
Where I sat with my tiger cat and greeted our guests.
Now they are back in their home—the forest.
I hear them but no longer see them.
Yet, they left part of their wilderness with me,
And for that I am thankful.

SPRING

Spring bursts forth with the truth
After being buried under winter's chill.
It is innocent and honest,
Looking for the perfect spot to grow:
With the soil supporting it...
And the sun encouraging it...
The seasonal rains nurturing it...
The growth is delicate yet hardy.
The moment is logical and magical,
While new, it is also ancient.
This truth of spring is part of our souls.
We must welcome it with an open heart.

MY MUSES

On this beautiful spring afternoon, I'm surrounded by furry muses.
The striped gray young cat Alice "the huntress" sits at my feet,
While encouraging my word flow, she suddenly needs to run up the tree.
Coco is the sleek "black panther" with his graceful moves—most of the time,
He pauses to observe me write, while his tail flits to a small bird's chirp.
Thunder the small-gray "clan elder" checks on my progress,
Then strolls off to sun herself in the distance while keeping a careful eye on me.
Rupert wearing his "gray tuxedo" is watching me, protectively perched in a window
He only looks away to kill an unwelcome houseguest, a pesky mosquito.
Chester lays on the deck's railing and he has my back under his watchful feral eyes,
This brown striped tiger shows no interest in the robin on the tree branch next to him.
Hermie, our "black lab," along with Sara, our "Shepherd blend,"
Rest comfortably in the house, but they would come to my aid
If any pesky deer or neighborhood dog dared approach me.
I have the blessings and protection of many furry muses.
These muses encourage me in their own special way,
And help ensure I record inner spring-thoughts into my journal.

SPRING DAY

It's too hot in the sun on this beautiful spring day
So I quickly relocate into the shade.
The wind gently blows a few clouds by...
The birds are scattered in the trees...
Their songs in surround sound...
The gentle tapping of the woodpecker
Reminding me of a blessing in Morse code.
My face has a permanent smile.
My mind at peace with the positive messages of nature.
My breaths are deep and relaxing.
My body calm as I find comfort on a lawn chair.
I'm surrounded by a grandfather-faced cedar...
And a single redwood bought as a gift.
Both have reached their space in the sky.
The maple and dogwoods are starting to bloom
The Douglas fir stands tall and proud
While the oak leans forward to get a perfect place
It is a time of rebirth and growth...
I feel that deep in my soul where it resides—on a spring day.

READY

Life is ready to resume when spring returns.
The bird's arrival means nests to be built.
The woodpecker continues cleaning the trees of bugs.
The hawks soar by looking for their next meal.
In the ground somewhere around me
Is a rabbit's den full of new lives?
The yellow jackets are making their muddy nests,
Especially around our doors.
The bear is back with its annual search for food.
We're reminded we are in raccoon territory,
Via our front door, leaving their strong scent behind.
Sometimes we get a whiff of skunk, signaling their arrival,
Although our dogs manage to find them, too.
The dogwoods bloom in large white flowers.
The bright green trees push higher toward the sun.
Green covers the soil for as long as the rains remain.
Everything is ready for the seasons of renewal…including me.

BEAUTIFUL DAY

I sit surrounded by unconditional love
It is a pure and patient place to exist
And I'm allowed to be me.
No judgments, fear, or hate here
Just beauty, joy, and wonder.
It is a place for my soul to dance in joyous wonder
Twirling, jumping, and spinning
Like the stars illuminated by the sun.
No arguments, hunger, or roles to play.
Only me in my own heaven—
In my front yard.
Only a glimpse of what is to come
But it is enough to keep me going
On this beautiful day and all those that follow.

SPLENDOR

Splendor abounds like an explosion of delicate fireworks
It is not only a visual treat but fills all my senses
The air so pure and clean from recent rains
As the growth of foliage follows
And the sun softly caresses my skin
While the gentle winds tease my hair.
The songs of the birds blend with the hum of bees
And the squawk of the squirrel provides the beats
...In this spring exhibition
I can taste the day in my soul
Filling all my hungers at every glance
I'm rewarded in this image of perfection
Yes, it a day of splendor
Going on whether we join it or not
Its invitation goes out to all
...I'll be there waiting for you
To join this sculpture of splendor.

PERFECTION

Vibrant...
Beautiful...
Inviting...
Its fragrance welcomes you
Making everything around it
Dull in comparison.
It's a splendor of—
Yellow, red, purple, white,
Orange, green, and blue.
It illuminates the world.
Delicate, yet strong.
It's bathed in the sun
It's nourished in rain
It's supported by the earth
Hummingbirds are drawn to it
The bees create from it
Humans capture images of it
It's nature's art—a limited edition.
Soon, the colors fade.
They wither on the branches.
They carelessly drop to the ground.
They become the balance that creates...more.
But this beauty's only temporary.
It's all there is and all it gives.
It is beauty, nourishment, and aroma.
The flower's gone as quickly as it appeared
But never completely forgotten
In a fleeting moment of petaled-perfection.

GREEN

Framed in the large window,
A spring day bursts forth in bright splendor.
A gentle breeze delivers it,
While the birds announce its arrival.
The berries labor in their blooms,
And the trees reach for the heavens.
The landscape is brought to life,
In the same fashion as a crayon
Wielded by a small child,
Determined to make it all—green.

BLOOMING

The world is blooming in color.
The sky frames it in a deep blue
A yellow glow caresses all that is seen
Including the sparkling trees,
In all the shades of green.

Even the dull brown of the tree bark,
More vibrant and alive.
But it is the ground
That has my attention.
In a framed picture of a brilliant flow.

There is a color explosion of:
Pink, red, orange, purple, blue, and yellow.
The flowers having created words,
They're written in nature's splendor.
An invitation to butterflies, bees, and hummingbirds.

A living celebration.
It's moving and changing, but
A few uninvited guests think it's their duty
To try to dampen the spirit of spring.
They can't, as they only nibble on its beauty.

This is our world—in its blooming glory.
I can't help but to pause,
Taking in this burst of color
In the only way I can, using words to access my soul
Happily pampered in nature's blooming—I could stay forever.

OUTSIDE

I step outside my door,
Heavy coat hung in the closet,
My arms bare
As they absorb the sun,
My legs and feet free
From boots and pants,
Sunglasses on my face.

I find a place to sit
To reflect on the new beauty,
The new life—
The gentle breeze,
The birds chirping,
The bees and butterflies,
Working around me.

The flowers have burst forth,
An abundance of color
Filling the air
With their sweet essence—
It is a quiet moment,
As I breathe it all in,
And reflect.

There is no chill in the air
As summer approaches,
A time of long days and swimming—
But for now, in spring,

I absorb the new season, and life,
As everything outside welcomes me,
And I, gleefully return the greeting.

SPRING GONE

Gone are the days when I lay on the couch
By the crackling wood stove
Huddled under a blanket with five cats...
Sleeping on or near me.

Gone are the cabin-fevered stares
Of cats who don't understand
When I tell them it's too cold outside...
It's snowing.

Gone are the silent crisp nights
When I have to convince
Our two dogs they need to go outside...
They can't hold it in all day.

Gone are the mornings
When I leave early to remove built-up snow
From my car's windshield...
And drive more carefully on the ice.

Gone are the times
When I sit in wonder.
Watching the landscape turn white...
In a beautiful dance of the snowflakes.

Gone is the silence of snow
And the soothing patter of rain
Or the roar of the wind...
Pounding its fury against the house.

Gone are those candlelit nights
When the outside rages on—
Gone are the coats, boots, hats, and mittens
All tucked away until next season.

These things are gone
But they are coming back
Until then I sit outside...
Surrounded by life.

The birds are singing,
And the crows screeching
As I catch the sweet scent of the flowers...
As a small fluffy cloud floats by.

The cats sit by me, again
Basking in the sun, along with my dogs
This will be gone soon, too...
When the leaves start to fall.

Each season is unique
In what it has to offer
Now, I'm blessed in a moment of spring...
In its blissful brilliance before—it is gone.

TENDING

When I step out my door
You are there…
Waiting for me.
You delicately fly past me,
Your black and yellow wings
Framed by spring's lushness
Circle once around me…
And then head off on your nectar hunt.
I water the potted plants…
Then move to another area
You are there, waiting.

You circle around me, again
As I tend your garden.
I say hello…
You fly close to my words
Then leave.
I feel like I have passed
The swallowtail butterfly's inspection
I anticipate high marks.
With a smile…
I go back to my tending
Knowing I will see you again.

BUTTERFLY

You linger by the front door.
You are always there
When I come out to water.
—You stay close.
Yet, not close enough to get wet.
I head to the backyard.
You are there
Anticipating my next move.
Your delicate yellow wings
Outlined in black, stay close.
You avoid the steady stream of water
As I direct the liquid of life
To the weeds that flower for you.
It's the least I can do,
For something that brings so much beauty
Into our world of blooming splendor
That only the butterfly can provide.

NEST

The nest took over the top of our gutter last spring
We awaited the chirps of baby birds...nothing.
The mother bird left the nest.
Days turned into weeks.
Maybe she built another nest somewhere else...
Curious, my ladder-perched husband looked at
Three intact tiny blue eggs, I was informed.
The fourth one was broken with dried yellow splatters.
Sad, we left them, unwilling to intrude
On the small promise that never happened
In the nest at the top of our gutter.

THE JOURNEY

The tiny brown and white bird clung to the cedar's bark
The corn snow fell heavy and hard around it.
Then, the bird slowly began its journey by climbing upward.
A few feet up the tree, it was knocked back down to the
  ground
It paused for only a few seconds and tried again.
Deliberately, it made its way back to where it fell
The tiny bird carefully passed that point without stopping
It moved higher, toward the promised shelter from the
  pounding chaos.
Wings open, it faltered a few times, but hung on…
It kept rising until it reached the first bare branch.
Tucked underneath, the little bird found limited shelter
But it wisely did not linger there as it continued the climb…
Finally, the brave bird is immersed into the green branches
Now it is safely nestled in the cedar, as the storm rages
  around it.
Gone from my sight now I contemplate its journey.
When the bird was knocked down it got up and tried again
It passed the point where it had been impeded
There was no hesitation as it kept advancing.
Not looking back, it climbed higher and higher.
It didn't accept the first offer of partial protection,
Instead it kept climbing until it reached its goal…
Until it found sanctuary from the pelting ice and winds.
And, having watched this journey—I was just a bit wiser for
  it

Because I knew whatever life threw at me, I needed to pick myself up
And keep climbing, no matter what the odds, until I reached the top
Exactly like the wise and brave bird did on its journey in the storm.

WALK

I was walking in the forest
The day was sweet with life
Beautiful, playful, and full of joy
I lightly hum in tune with my step
I'm smiling and free.
Across my path a shadow crosses.
I pause,
I hesitate,
I see nothing.
Again, I begin my journey
Happy in my thoughts,
Without fear or stress.
I hear a sound.
It is right above me.
But I see it, too late.
Frozen in my steps, I can't stop it,
As it crashes down on me.
The pain is unbearable,
Yet, I'm still alive.
Trapped, I'm its prisoner.
Scared, I try to call out.
Nothing escapes my lips.
I'm alone...
As the skies darken.
Where there was life...
Now, there is silence.
There is no one there to help me.

My fears increase,
As my life is a distant memory.
In that moment, everything changed.
There was nothing I could do to stop it.
As I push and pull it makes no difference,
Except to cause more pain.
Finally, I stop fighting.
I wait for the end...
Believing it is all I have left.
Then, I glance above me and see it.
A glimmer of light.
Hope.
Faith.
Love.
My fight is back.
Each movement is agony
Yet, I am moving.
I slowly inch away from my jail
Finding an escape route,
I am poked and prodded
By its wooden prison bars.
I find I'm not broken,
Just bruised and scratched.
Encouraged, I continue,
After what seems like days
I am free.
The weight is now gone,

I'm battered and bruised.
But I pull myself up...
Until I'm tall and proud.
I'm able to continue my walk
Through the peace and joy.
Each step brings the song back.
I glance back at the old dead tree.
It should have killed me, but it didn't.
My body is hurt, but healing.
I step over a part of that tree
And continue my walk.
Back into the day—filled with life
Less bounce in my step
But not in my heart.
I smile.
And I feel whole again.
Where I'm supposed to be.
I lightly step over the debris littering the forest floor
And wonder if others are trapped like I was.
I don't see them, but I feel they are there.
I send them love.
So perhaps they will realize they can still walk.
They are okay.
It's just life...
It's just life...
Keep walking.

UNDERWATER WORLD

I enter reverently
Into the quiet world.
Blue surrounds me
As I draw my breath
Through a plastic tube.

My vision protected
Behind a tight mask...
Waterproof camera in hand
I propel myself forward
With my pink fins.

I am quickly greeted
By curious butterfly fish...
The sea's welcoming committee.
We make eye contact
Both equally curious.

Floating in the moment
Time stands still
And I am part
Of this underwater world.
I snap a picture as a reminder.

In a domain of beauty
I swim forward
As an honored guest.
But I am careful...
Not to wear out my welcome.

WAVES

The waves glide smoothly on top
Of the salty surface, proudly...
Blending against the azure
Until they merge together profoundly.

Their roar precedes them...
As they hit land—this is where it ends...
They are positive, but they are wrong...
That was only their birth, now the journey begins.

PARADISE

The tropical leaves blow gentle in the wind.
They circulate the heavy, salty air.
The waves crash against the lava stones.
The black crab picks through the ocean's offering.
Looking for a meal, a red bird flies above.
Then delicately, it rests on a white floral branch.
A lone cloud floats by and pauses above me.
The landscape goes quiet with anticipation
Then the cloud spills liquid life onto the lush landscape
While the sun bares down creating a rainbow.
It is a brief beautiful moment...
Until the tropic breeze pushes it away.
The bird on the branch begins its song.
The palm leaves swaying to their melody.
The crab is still searching, claws reaching...
The waves continue crashing onto the stones
Each motion and movement in a harmonious blend.
All in a place of perfection called paradise.

THE LINE

Feeling like a duck
I float on top of the salty surface.
My breath coming from above
My attention pinned below.
I'm balanced on the line
Between air and water.
Pink fins push me forward
Until I come across a school of fish.
The fish are yellow and white striped
As they gently flow by me.
They are looking for sustenance
With a bigger fish following.
I ponder if he is their protector
Or are they his meal?
I shrug, floating above all of this life
Knowing I'm a small part of the vast.
It is a silent place—peaceful
That completely accepts me.
I come to a patch of purple coral
Shaped like a brain.
I see the ocean's deep wisdom there
Of being what and where it needs to be.
Just like I am
On both sides of the line.

SNORKELERS

Everyone on the shore has applied their suntan lotion.
They have found a place for their towel to wait for them.
They scan the horizon to see where everyone has gone.
They find where people are floating on their stomachs,
People breathing through tubes gathered in groups.
Convinced there is much to see through peering eyes,
Swimmers gear up...mask on heads...snorkels dangling.
The final touch: fins put on amongst the waves,
Swimmers plod confidently forward with one final stare.
Then they fall forward into the ocean and swim.
Mask firmly covering eyes and nose, snorkel in mouth.
Swimmers see what the others have been seeing.
It is a world of color beneath the waves.
A paradise only offered to these snorkelers.

PEACEFUL MOMENT

It's been so long—
My mind races for things to do...
I ignore it.
Instead I settle down into my ocean view.
I'm perched above the people-filled pool.
Palm trees gently swaying around me.
The surging surf attracts my attention
Wave after wave reaches out to hypnotize me
It deposits its essences onto the rocky shore.
My shoulders...slacken
My attention...absolved
My soul...smiles.
In this tropical paradise
I only have to be and observe
To become a part of it
In this peaceful moment at the sea.

PARROTS

With a full stomach I watch the sun set.
I sit quietly enjoying the peace.
Suddenly, a flock of birds breaks the silence.
A lone bird breaks off from the group.
It perches in the palm tree in front of me.
It squawks loudly, as more birds fill the sky
The moving wave directly overhead.
Another bird detaches and lands in the same tree.
They are green with a long tail—a parrot, I realize.
Hundreds, maybe thousands of birds saturate the sky.
It is the parrots nightly trek to find shelter I quickly find out.
As the sun disappears, they bounce from tree to tree.
Soon the sky is empty, and the trees are full.
Quiet takes over the landscape again into the night,
Until dawn breaks through the peaceful slumber.
The birds are alerted it is time to leave.
It's time to search for food.
With the same loud ruckus they arrived in,
They take to the air and form a flock again.
In awe, I watch these parrots of Kauai.
And each night there, I eagerly await their return.

STARK

It is a stark scene offered below
The whiteness camouflaging the blue beneath.
It appears safe and solid like a snowy country spread.
A place you'd relax by a fire on a winter's chilly eve.
Yet, you're able to rip through the landscape.
There's no resistance in these valleys and hills.
It's all but an illusion shackled with liquid,
Releasing its prisoner by raining down upon reality.
For now though—you're beyond it all in an airplane.
Above the starkness found in the realm of clouds.

CLOUDS

On top of the clouds...
I float in a metal bird.
The sea is speckled...
Like sprinkles on a cake.
My space is limited...
But the beauty below abounds.
The roar of the engine...
Doesn't cover the shrill of the small child.

The icy air pours down on me...
Until I close the small vent.
Insert my earplugs...
And go into my own world.
With Pink Floyd narrating...
I am in a place between worlds.
Where I can find the space...
That poetry lives—above the clouds.

ERUPTION

Everyone eagerly clusters in the marked spot
Cameras out snapping shot after shot.
In the distance the lava flows.
I take my picture, ready to move on.
Instead, I sit. I watch.
The red glow moving, changing.

While the smoke surges upward.
This constant motion of liquid earth
Was more than just a photo op.
It was a volcano forming:
Rock, land, and island.
In this eruption I witnessed—
A new creation and continuation of life.

BE

The wind sways through the palm trees,
Gently cooling the warm humid air.
As the ocean rumbles and crashes
Onto the sandy shore.

A tiny brown bird perches
On the balcony railing.
You observe each other,
As it hops to the ground.

It searches for food you missed
Before flying back to the palm tree.
Your peace has been found
In the moment, you connected.

You breathe it all in
Knowing you can *be* present
To take everything in—
Just like the small brown bird.

ENCOUNTER

You appear so delicate, so fragile
I hear the familiar hum of your wings
You dart from flower to flower
You grace my feeder with your presence
Your long beak searches...
It searches for the sweetness of life's nectar
You take your fill of nature's colorful bounty
You fill your tiny, feather-covered body
You are perfection in the air
Then there is that moment
That moment when you stop and watch me
Our eyes meet and it's as if our souls touch
I feel the sweetness that fills you
It spills over onto me in joy and happiness
The connection is broken as you fly off
But, my smile is intact as I go back to my life
I have an extra bounce in my step
From my brief encounter with—a hummingbird.

HUMMINGBIRD

You fly through my flowers
Your wings appear motionless
You move with a grace to the feeder
You dine, but before you leave…
I find you observing me
The doorway is a place to enter
Or a place of exit, but you do neither
It becomes a place of visceral reflection
And this manifestation moment is eternal
Here we meet in the soft silence
Our eyes connect—human and hummingbird
Suspended in our own dimension
Where thoughts spontaneously merge and mingle
This is instantaneous and endless in this space
Suddenly you break the spell and fly away
Yet, a part of you stayed behind with me
And hopefully a part of me flew off with you
I feel enlightened in a way that I can't explain
But it doesn't matter as I go back to my life,
My step is lighter, and my soul's soaring in the sky.

WATERFALL

You tumble down trusting and brave…
To your destination.
Following and leading with the same result…
Your roar rings out.
Your battle cry, your confidence…
It's the same thing.
You slowly etch away your surroundings…
With your force.
Yet, all I can do is watch your magnificence…
Your beauty—my gift.
I snap picture after picture on my camera…
Stilling that one moment.
I plan to share it on Facebook to reflect my travels…
While you never stop.
You keep rushing in your roaring glory…
And I am grateful.
I have been a brief witness of your perfection…
I can only offer my thanks.

THE SMELL

I open the door to let the cats out.
They pause and smell the air.
Showing their displeasure they refuse to move.
I frown, wondering, until the scent finds my nose.
I immediately find the source—our front door's bottom.
Finally, the cats leap over the door frame.
I get to cleaning wondering about the mystery animal,
We are obviously in its territory with the pungent scent left behind.
I investigate on the internet. Fox, coyote, mountain lion…?
Determined to figure out this mystery…
I repoint the security camera toward the front door and wait.
Night after night, nothing until that one moment,
When the camera captures the offender.
He carefully waddles up to our angel fountain.
Here, he stops and starts drinking.
But what he does next is my answer.
He makes a stop at the front door.
This raccoon leaves a memento of his visit.
Striped tail and mask reflect his outlaw behavior.
Mystery solved as I snap a quick picture.
The next morning, I rinse off the front door again.
But, is his behavior that of a criminal,
Or perhaps he considers us a part of his extended family?
Where his mark offers his generous protection for water.
Does that mean he expects the same from us?
I can only give him our vinegar-smell.
I hope he understands that it's my respect right back.

THE CALL

We wait patiently perched on our lounges.
No lights on—as the stars encase us.
Blankets protect us from the night chill.
Bottles of water beside us.
Black flashlight in my lap, just in case.
We don't have to wait long to be rewarded.
The first meteor streaks across the sky.
"Oh! There's one!" I exclaim.
It's like a wish is being granted.
Then it disappears behind the trees and darkness returns.
Again, we wait in peaceful silence, my husband and I.
We both try not to fall asleep and miss anything.
A sudden strange sound from beyond our fence.
It calls and calls and calls...
I bravely shine the light in the direction of the shrill.
I peer into the dark trying to locate the creature, nothing.
The calls start again. This time there's a distant response.
Finally, the darkness grows quiet again.
More meteors light up the sky with their golden streaks.
The only witnesses are us and the forest animals.
Soon sleep wins and we venture back into the house.
My husband goes to bed and I investigate that sound.
My computer screen is blindingly bright at first.
Soon, I have it narrowed down to a fox.
The fox mating call with the expected response.
Quite an adventure for us and those foxes...
During the meteor shower on a dark summer night.

DRAGONFLY

The orange dragonfly is perched on a dead branch.
Motionless…It watches me silently.
It greets me each day as I water the garden.
My tiny guest is quiet…
Unless it soars off with another dragonfly.
Then next day it's in the same spot, waiting.
Sometimes it will fly by my face,
As if to reassure me it's still here.
Then, it settles back down to watch me—
Blesses the branch making sure I tend its plants.
I fill the birdbath last leaving water for all its guests.
The dragonfly is one of nature's magical hosts
That graces my garden—and I am glad.

PORCH GIFT

I step out the front door narrowly escaping the gift—
An unmoving mouse.
It has been carefully placed for me
By one of our cats, with love and pride,
Letting me know I'm held in high regard.
My furry family offers the product of their hunt.
It's presented beautifully next to our welcome mat.
I wait for the cats to come in for the night,
To carefully place this gift left on our porch,
In a large green container with weekly pickup.
I watch my step knowing there could be more,
But more importantly I know I'm loved.

SENTRY

She sits alert, watching.
Yet, indifferent at the same time.
Tail twitching she spots a bumblebee.
When the black and yellow nectar-gatherer leaves.
And the striped sentry loses interest.
Instead, she studies a plastic flower.
Again her attention fades.
Finally something peaks her curiosity.
A fake blue butterfly...
Spinning around a green-leaf cloth plant.
This solar motion comes under attack.
She wrestles the moving garden decoration...
Until satisfied it offers no danger.
Tail held high she gracefully moves on.
She settles down onto the lawn watching.
Her pink nose sniffs the air...
But her green eyes are pinned on the forest.
She keeps her hunter stance for a few moments.
Then, she carefully makes her way back to me.
She adds in a small meow as she lays at my feet.
Patiently she waits to be petted for a job well done...
As the sentry of the garden—and forest.

THE SONG

When the bee sang, I stood alone.
The sun bared down on me,
As I stopped to admire the flowers.
I heard a song—pure and innocent
Like an angel singing to me.
There were no words only voice.
In awe I listened and scanned the flowers.
Soon, I saw a lone honeybee fly away.
Maybe, I wondered, just maybe...
It was a miracle just for me.

AWE

I'm above the tall lily stalks.
The delicate orange tubes
Are bursting with nectar.
They reach hungerly for the sun.

A heavy cement turtle guards them.
As a mother reads to a child
In plastic perfection.
A rock-rabbit is heavy, yet alert.

White roses fill the empty space.
They spill their fragrance carelessly
Where an extortionary bee is collecting pollen.
In this scene nestled in the moment.

I pause taking it all in.
Expecting a gentle hum of a bee
But instead I am greeted in song.
It's a beautiful feminine voice.

"Laaaaaaaa..."
It's like nothing I've heard before
Puzzled, I look for the source and find it.
It is not a radio or TV, but a simple bee.

Alone in my awe, I shake my head at this curiosity.
Had the song always been there, I pondered,
Buried under work, chores, and life? I was baffled.
Had I experienced a miracle? Yes! I realized...yes!

SONG

I took a break from yard work.
I stood on our dry redwood deck.
My gaze flowed over the lush landscape.
Pausing at the orange flowers beneath...
I breathed in the quiet peace.
I soaked in the soothing sun.
Then, I heard it.
A sweet high voice carried to me.
I wonder if a neighbor's radio is on.
I carefully search for the sound.
I'm surprised by what I find.
It's a simple honeybee,
In a honeyed voice singing "la, la, la..."
Each note was pure in the sweet-space.
I'm spellbound. Finally, I'm able to speak.
I call to my husband, "You have to hear this!"
The bee flees the moment he's next to me.
We search the garden for this bee, without luck.
He smiles at my story and goes back to his chores.
I smile back. Someday I will meet this bee again,
The bee that sang like an angel...
Amongst the flowers—apparently just for me.

THE DAY AFTER

A lone blue jay shrieks loudly.
The gentle wind blows the heat.
And the sun finds me...
As I find the shade.
My cat rubs against my legs.
The neighbor's air conditioner hums.
A fly zooms by like a fighter jet
While the vibrant butterflies tend the flowers.
Though the silence underneath
Still lurks from the day before.
When a bee's hum turned into song.
It reminded me to look beyond what I see,
Past what I feel...
Remember what I had forgotten.
All in that small space of time...
In the peace of the bee's song
...the day after.

MIRACLE

Yesterday I was given a miracle
Standing on my deck.
A beautiful song reached my ears
Like a small angel holding a sweet note.
All in a moment of a still summer day.
A radio was my first thought.
But the sound moved as the bee did
Tending the flowers.
It wasn't humming as it worked—
It sang.

In that moment my stress was gone
My fears abated.
The list of things to do vanished
And worries and pain disappeared.
All I had was the song.
It was gone as quickly as it came.
But the feeling remained
The little bee had reminded me.
What was important and all I had to do—
Was listen to the miracle.

SCARED

I rushed into the darkness
My cell phone in the car
Needing to be charged before slumber.
Flashlight in hand, I made it to the vehicle.
I quickly found my link to the world.
I also grabbed the large inner tube
That we used that day swimming at the lake.
That's when I heard a loud snapping sound.
It came from the darkness, in the trees.
Startled, I shined my flashlight toward the noise.
There was a small black bear climbing a tree.
Below, our garbage strewn everywhere.
My first thought was to take a picture.
Using my flashlight to illuminate it,
As the cinnamon bear scooted higher.
With barely any battery left on my cell, I got the shots.
A warning growl and I removed the light's glare.
He only wanted to be left alone on the cedar.
I honored that and hurried back into the house.
I knew I hadn't been scared of the bear.
I'd walked right past it in the darkness.
I was only armed with my flashlight.
But, upon my return there was a plastic pink donut.
That was the tipping point of what scared it.
What pushed it up the tree to escape the water toy.
The tube had increased my scary girth to that bear.

I smiled at my encounter as indoor lights greeted me.
Even with the knowledge of the garbage clean up.
I ran into one small black bear who wanted nothing to do
With a large blow-up toy that scared it from its meal.

A CLOUD

A cloud slowly floats by.
It appears as a screaming face.
It alarms me.
My heart starts to race...
My body tenses...
My breath pauses.
Then, the image dissipates.
It's carried away by a gentle wind.
Only blue sky is left...
A chill shot through me.
Was a message in that silent scream?
Did it represent my hurt and pain?
Perhaps, I thought...perhaps.
I pondered that warm summer day
Watching the skies fill with fluffy clouds.
Why did I see that?
Was it my role as the well-adjusted adult,
Still have dreams screaming to be let out?
Or was it my frustrated buried innocence?
A bird startles me, gliding to another tree.
It crosses the path where the cloud had been.
I wonder...maybe...just maybe...
While the trees swayed gently.
What if that cloud was a reminder...
To let my painful memories dissipate.
Let them float into my own blue skies.

A place where the sun shines brightly.
Where I can soar once more like the bird.
Those silent screams would be gone.
Could I let them go like a cloud in the sky?
I could...I think...if I allow it to happen.

DRAGONFLY'S TRAP

By the front door a spider spun a delicate web.
I pass by amazed by its size, design, and beauty.
One day I'm leaving with my grandson.
He immediately spots a dragonfly stuck in it.
"Is it dead?" he asks.
"Looks like it," I reply.
But it wiggles, so rescue ensues,
With another dragonfly keeping careful watch.
Soon, the orange dragonfly is freed from its trap.
My grandson and I are pleased
As the two dragonflies fly safely away.
The next day the large intricate web is back,
And so is the orange dragonfly.
It greets me as I go outside while avoiding the web.
I know the dragonfly is grateful—
And the spider had understood, its bounty unlimited
By my front door where it spins its web.

THE HUNTRESS

She hides under the deck
Using it as her private fortress
Unmoving, her green eyes
Survey the landscape.

She peeks out
Only to retreat
Finally, it's time
She steps into the sunlight.

Crouched low to the ground
Each step placed in silence
As her tail gently sways
And her ears are straight and alert.

She delicately sniffs the air
Satisfied, she continues toward a rock
She rubs against it
And moves on.

Soon, she is immersed in the green grass
A fly dares to go near her
She pounces, but misses
She moves undeterred to the large cedar.

Her presence is noted by a squirrel
He loudly chirps his displeasure
But she ignores him, as she cleans her gray fur
A bird flies by, and lands on a low branch.

Her attention shifts
She makes her way toward that perch
The bird watches her approach
As the striped huntress pounces.

The wise bird takes flight
But the huntress is not discouraged
As she valiantly makes her way
To the deck railing to bask in the sun.

Her eyes closed as her tail swishes
Displaying her alertness
If any prey venture across her path
For now, the huntress rests.

WIND

The wind gently glides through the metal chimes
Bringing a sweet sound while the cedar releases its seeds.
These seeds twirl down like tiny helicopters.
The oak tree's leaves slide gently to the ground.
The air is cool—at least for today,
As the blue jays empty the bird feeder.
Small puffy white clouds float free in the blue sky.
The roses are blooming colors and fragrance.
The spiders still spinning their webs.
But a change is coming soon.
As the heat of summer dissipates,
And autumn pushes its way in with its red and orange.
It's a final push of a late summer's cooling wind.

THUNK

The wind is blowing fall into summer,
With a thunk, thunk hitting the deck.
The trees are starting to release,
For the season's change.
It's a loud transition.
It's heard by the insects, birds, and animals
As they make their final preparations.
The air is cooler at night,
The days growing shorter.
Air conditioners exchanged for heaters.
Sweaters pulled from the closet at twilight.
As the thunk of fall approaches...
Today I will enjoy the end of summer.

HEAR

I'm watching the stars warm the summer night.
I hear you booming through the forest.
The night goes silent...
I turn to the sound when a branch crackles.
You hear me...you stop.
I observe the darkness.
Tension fills the air for an instant.
We share the same air and time
While peering into the night.
We are frozen in the moment.
I only feel your curiosity, not aggression.
So I move first, snapping more branches.
You loudly run off into the dark.
I couldn't tell what you were...
Only what my imagination showed me.
Bear, deer or...but we are both safe.
We are shadows passing each other,
With no harm between us.
I had always been safe perched above you
And you always protected from me on my deck.
If only that applied all the time
Outside this moment, outside this forest
What a world this would be...if only.

NATURE
Fall and Winter

GLOW

The forest is aglow with fall.
The reds, pinks, and golds overtaking green.
It blends together under the blue sky.
While sun's rays accentuate the creation.
The dogwoods, ash, and cottonwood trees
Demand attention to their beauty...
In a glittery fall flash.
Before brown, gray, and white winter
Takeover in an icy-chilling clench.
It is a time of beauty...
A time of change...
A time to prepare...
A time to walk amongst this glow.
To know it's the end of growing season
When life bursts through a cold spring ground.
Now it's a firework of leaves brightly blazing.
But before they disappear you can't help being that kid
Who kicks the pile of leaves or picks up a red leaf.
During the last eruption of fall's glow.

RED

Outside my kitchen window,
The dogwood trees light up the forest.
In their golden-pink and red splendor,
It is startling against the deep green.
Just like the bloom of a flower,
It is a temporary but satisfying pleasure.
Soon, the leaves will scatter on the land,
And the trees will stand brown and bare.
The chill of the impeding winter,
And their hibernation is coming.
But for now they give us,
The beauty of a red fall.
Where magic abounds...
And memories happen...
Where each walk is special...
And every glance rewarded...
When the nights are cooler...
And the days are growing shorter...
This is the gift of fall.
Not only a time to harvest our crops,
But harvest our perceptions.
This will carry us over until spring,
When the landscape bursts into life again.
But for now we enjoy the encore of beauty,
In the stunning red hue that flows from fall.

FALL

It comes in gently at first,
Coloring the world in orange, yellow, and red...
Filling the pathways with its piles.
They are only meant to be kicked through—
In youthful abandonment.
But, the rains weigh it all down
Making it time to clean up...
Until the pathways are barren and sterile.
Then winter brings a colorless time,
When pale ice falls from the sky.
But now there is fall and harvest.
A time to rejoice and embrace everything,
Before settling into a long winter rest.

LEAVES

The leaves not only provide for the trees,
But the birds, squirrels, insects, and humans, too.
They come out brightly in spring's growth.
Then in summer, grant us shade.
The fall is when they produce a show.
Starring: splendor and solitude
With special effects engineered by:
Anticipation and abundance.
The ground crew navigates the final flight...
Of the colorful leaves' journey to earth.
Preparing the audience for the chill of winter
And the icy breath that signals respite.
Yet, it is the leaves motion picture
That carefully choreographs each step.
Show us that life can be beautiful at any stage.
As I watch this spell-binding production,
I ponder my own stage of life...
Knowing what can be learned from the leaves
As I prepare for my own winter like the foliage.

CRISP

The nights are quiet and crisp.
The air is filled with autumn's colors.
An incoming storm fills the sky,
With a promise of things to come.
Of change...
Of rest...
Of harvest...
Of abundance.
It is all there in the air.
Crisp, almost icy
As we wait for a season.
One that brings us...
Not only transformation, but faith.

POETRY

A moment for which poetry is written
Is in the heavy misty mornings.
The silence only interrupted
By the rain-laden pine and oak branches
As they release their burdens.
The earth gladly receives them.
The air is filled with crisp anticipation
Of the solitary season's approach.
Trees in the distance lay sleeping in the fog.
The skies are gray and heavy with moisture.
The dogwood trees on the edge of the world...
Filled with red, pink, and gold.
Smoke fills the air, but not from forest fires.
Instead, it's woodstoves heating the homes.
The dogs don't linger on their first morning outing.
I smile and pull my coat tighter around me
The heat of summer has faded into a memory
As autumn greets me like an old friend
These are the mornings that poetry blooms.

MIST

The day is cold and gray.
The air crisp and moist.
As I venture outside,
Gone are my shorts and sleeveless shirts.
They're replaced by sweaters and sweats.
The sun is tucked behind the clouds.
Mist swaddles the trees in a fog of splendor—
Distant mountains, hidden under precipitation.
I breathe it all in deeply.
Noting the air is filled with autumn.
The dogwoods, ash, and maples,
Replacing green with reds and yellows.
It is a lull in the storms.
It is a time of in-between.
Between the sun baking the earth
Or the forest being covered in ice.
It is a perfect time for harvest.
For celebration…
For apples and pumpkins…
For beauty.
All brought in on a mist…
On a glorious morning in autumn.

TREES

My soul sways like the trees,
Both rooted firmly in the ground.
Water pours out of the sky.
The winds pound furiously.
Trees bending, but not breaking.
They ride the storm out.
Then, in the silence, the snow.
A temporary frozen situation.
That soon disappears back into fall.

The sun surges forth.
Warming the icy branches.
The birds slowly appear...
The animals emerge...
Humans make their way...
Into the deep forest.
Like my soul—in my own storm
The day when that storm passes
And I wait—like the trees
For that moment in the sun.

RAIN

Each drop races to the ground
There is no letting up
Each drop more determined
Than the last—to win.
There is no hiding from nature's games
Even when you are warmly tucked inside.
Like the hibernating bears—
Full stomach and sleepy eyes.
The rain keeps coming.
Relentless in its goal to win the game.
Its strength compares to that small insect
That eats away at your house's foundation
Bit by bit until it wins.

TIME

When time changes over from the bustle of the heat
To the calm of the cold, when things move outside to in.
Clothing protects me from the chill of nature.
No demands are requested from the garden.
Only the wood stove asks for my attention.
Warm drinks, filling meals, comfy couches...
Are there now, because it is time to renew.
To rest because all the work is done for now.
I am ready to sit and enjoy my harvest.
It is time to reflect, to embrace and rest.
As the freeze of winter stalks me, I let it.
Welcome it in—for not only do bears need this.
I need to rest and renew and now, I have the time.
And I will gladly take what is offered to me.

GRAY

The sun is gone.
It has been for some time.
The drab grayness blankets your world.
It keeps you inside waiting and watching.
It is heavy and moist. It presses you down.
You can't crawl out, yet you find a space.
It's comfortable and calming, too.
You burrow deep into the gray cocoon,
Waiting for the radiance's arrival.
And the gray lifts away...
You may even miss the sluggish stillness.
But the gray will fade away into the sun, again.

STORM

I have waited for you.
It has been so long since we last met.
I looked for you in the past
But I couldn't find you.
Did you know that?
I worried I'd never see you again.
Now you unleash your powers
While I am safely tucked inside,
Completely amazed at your dominance.
I have missed you.
How you transform everything you touch.
In fact, you define what change is,
In each gust of wind...
Every drop of rain...
Or individual snowflake...
Nothing is ever the same—
When the blue skies return.
I don't mind the storm
No matter what you bring.
Because without you
There would be no life.
I smile and enjoy the show.

IMMERSE

I immerse myself into the storm.
Its power engulfs me,
As it cleanses my soul
With a brush of existence.

Ruling firmly without warning,
It is a delicate balance between
What it can give—
And what it can take away.

I connect to this authority
Its winds, rain, and snow rule
It is the same inside me
With my hidden emotions.

I'm immersed in the eye of the storm.
As it rages around and in me.
I wait for the calm,
Safe where I am at the moment.

Soon the sun will shine
My soul will be whole again.
But until then I welcome…
This healing immersion into the storm.

TREMBLES

Mt. Shasta
You sit in the distance
Covered in white splendor
Touching the clouds.

On the blue horizon
You are silent and strong
Pushing your way to the top.

You sit in judgment of those below
Until that day—
When you pass your sentence.

Your fury and rage
Will rain down upon us—
We pretend that day won't come.

Yet it will—
When the mountain trembles
We are out of time for truth.

BURIED

The sun is out.
It can't warm the land
Buried deep beneath the snow.
A pine stands out—green and brown.
Under it a lone squirrel digs.

He can't find his buried treasure.
The gray squirrel gives up.
Then he finds my small gift.
Small birds searching for food
Steal dog kibbles from our garage.

The children's slide is unused.
It's covered in a frosty layer,
Like a turtleneck sweater.
The whitened roof reflects purity
And absorbs the light from above.

It is a peaceful time to relax and enjoy.
Until it is time for all that is hidden
To be revealed, but for now it stays
Concealed under all that white…
Until spring nurtures what is buried.

A STORM

Heavy air whooshes through the trees.
It groans its creaky complaint.
But birds are sheltered...
Squirrels hidden...
Bears asleep...
They know a storm is coming.
I welcome and resist these soaking rains.
As they bring life, they can bring flood.
Flowing...
Flowing...
As the winds jolt the tall pines, they bend or break.
We survive these storms, awaiting the sun's return.

THE TREE

It pushes through the hard ground
Stretching and reaching...
For the brightness beyond.
The tree competes for its spot
Unsure what it will find.
The rain and sun nurture it.
It pushes on past others...
Those who didn't make it.
Then the snow comes,
Weighing the tree down.
Some branches snap under pressure.
Some trees break in half.
But the growing tree stays strong.
It waits for the thaw...
For the warmth of the sun.
Soon the snow turns to rain.
The sun warms the forest.
The tree keeps growing...
Past the bigger trees that fell.
The days grow longer.
The animals have returned.
A bird lands on its branch.
The tree feels its usefulness.
A nest rests carefully in its boughs.
Shortly, eggs hatch under a loving mother.
A squirrel claims the tree as home.

Pinecones fill its branches.
Growing like the baby birds,
Quickly though, they are both gone.
The scorching heat bears down.
The ground is dry—everything parched.
While the tree waits for the rains again.
The cycle repeats itself—there is a new tree.
It's reaching for the same sky the big tree graces.
The tree stands guard over the baby trees.
It protects and nurtures the best it can.
Finally, that first drop hits the thirsty ground.
Soil soaks up life, while the new tree sips from it.
It reaches…
It grows…
It thrives…
Roots spreading outward, while anchoring deeply.
As the new tree reaches for the promised light.

PLANT

Pinecones are scattered on the ground
On a bed of brown pine needles.
Small green plants push through to the sun.
The forest is mindful now of longer days
While its winter floor is still saturated
With the precious gift from beyond the canopy.
Soon, the woods will be ablaze in colors
As the forest comes alive again with growth.
It's a gentle reminder that as winter leaves
It's time to plant our minds with love.
Let it grow in all the seasons of our lives.

RAIN

The rain beats down
It is heavy and loud
Like a drum rhythm
Over and over.

Nothing is safe from it
As it plays its song
On everything in its path
Beautiful and demanding.

It is impossible to live without
Yet, its strength brings danger
In its tempo...
In its intensity.

Water is everything we need
And everything we don't—
It doesn't care either way
For now it is just rain.

A DOG'S STARE

You stare at me…
"Do you want to go outside?" I ask.
You answer with a whine as confirmation.
I throw on a coat and take you into the chill.
You stare at me…
You smell the air, sit, and wait.
I know your trick, though, I wait, you wait.
Nothing. I bring you back inside with me.
You're surprised I didn't leave you outside.
I know you can climb over the fence—barely.
I don't want you to roam the neighborhood.
I know you want to visit, play, and explore.
You don't realize standing in the middle of the road…
And watching the cars drive by isn't a good thing.
No one wants to stop and say hi to the cute black lab.
Back inside I sit down and go back to writing.
You stare at me…
You whine…
I don't bother to ask if you need to go. I sigh, grabbing my coat.
This time you finally do what you needed to on the lawn.
You sniff the air longingly one more time, but we go back
  inside.
You lay safely by the fire, but soon it will begin all over again.
That is until your wandering urge passes—or it is raining.
Right now, though, I go back to my words and you to your nap.
That is until you stare at me again…

WARMTH

In the warmth of a winter day
I sit perched on the edge of the forest
Arms exposed to the purity of the moment
My ears filled with the song of the woods
My lungs deeply absorb the beauty
Rain and snow a distant memory
As the sun bathes the landscape
And I enjoy the warmth of this day
Until winter makes its promised return.

THE MISSING CAT

I was right there only feet away from you.
Across the street on our neighbor's property.
I called out...you answered.
You didn't run away, yet I couldn't get you.
I didn't know what to do.
We were separated by a barbed wired fence.
I called and called then I sat down.
I hoped you'd come to me.
All we did was look at each other.
I searched for a way around to you.
I thought you would stay and wait.
Walking through the forest around the fence,
I alerted the new neighbor and found your spot.
But you weren't there!
Frantically, I searched and searched.
I couldn't find you, my chance gone.
The day was gone now, and I stopped looking.
But your eyes haunted me as I tried to sleep.
I still hear your meows replying to me...
The next day I looked again.
My breath visible as I called you.
There was no reply.
I look for clues of your existence.
The frosty towering trees offered no help.
I envisioned you cold, hungry, and scared.
You weren't even my cat, only visiting us.

My visitors had to leave. "I would find her," I assured.
So, you didn't know where you were, and another day gone.
You were in a strange place filled with ice and snow.
Days of searching passed, then someone ate the food left out.
Hope was raised again. The traps were set filled with food.
The next morning...nothing...another day...nothing.
The traps were set again.
This new morning we were greeted with a capture.
We got you back thin, scared, but safe.
A housecat now wise to the ways of the forest.
She still visits us, but she only observes the outdoors.

NIGHT CALLS

The night calls you, with sounds I can't hear.
You answer back, breaking the silence.
Disturbing any sleep around you.
I remind you to be quiet...you forget.
We go outside, and you stare at the fence.
You smell the air, then you go back inside.
You lie down wagging your tail. I lay down, too.
We sleep, until the night calls out...and you answer.
No one sleeps when you reply to the night calls.

MUSING FROM THE
BACK OF A HARLEY

MUSINGS

The winds blow our cares away
The rumble announces our presence
As we move forward to nowhere
We enjoy the view as we go
It is our occasion of peace
We are wrapped in leather cocoons
My hand tightly clasps a blue notebook
Its tan pages protesting the winds
I rest it on my husband's back
And tightly clutch my blue pen
While balanced on the back of the bike
We're emerged in a wall-less wonder
While the words pour forth from my soul
I attempt to make sense of this experience
A carefree moment of an aged-youth...
Of what I now call:
Musings from the Back of a Harley

THE OCTOBER SUN

The October sun bleeds through the trees
Clotting up before it reaches me.
The wind is a chilling reminder that I'm alive.
And it's the end of a day...
On a ride through the tall pines and cedars.
It's the end of the weekend...
As we race the impeding darkness home.
Ending in a grateful moment...
Existing in the changing blood-tinted landscape,
Dripping its beauty upon my eyes in memories.
I am at peace with myself and the changes.
In a time when my body and nature
Surge through each other, flowing and ebbing.
Feeling the grip of autumn in my bones
I welcome it all as we pass a house...
Decorated for the coming holiday
In spiders, tombs, pumpkins, and ghosts.
This is an October ride...on the back of a Harley.

FALL RIDE

The landscape is filled with tall evergreens.
Red peeks through winking at us.
Temporary signs on the side of the street…
Offer apples, pies, and cider to hungry travelers.
The air is chilled in anticipation…
Of winter's coming frost.
Riding through the changing scene…
I realized I'm changing with it.
Carefree in my moment…
Before the holidays.
I remember.
I remember I'm grateful to be here.
Seeing all the changes…
And becoming them, too.

WORTH

The day was heavy in gloom
The distance shrouded in gray.
The blue masked from my eyes
As we blew forward on the Harley
Toward a bright blue lake.
I do not smell any difference.

Riding through this smoke
Today is better my cell phone assured.
I wonder as we boldly keep going
With the trees green
The ground solid and firm.
The sun warms me.

Surrounded by the smoke
From the fires of California.
Was this ride worth it?
Yes, I think as we come to the lake
The gray gloom has lifted
And the smell is gone.
There are the clear waters of Lake Tahoe.

Blue pours forth in all directions
It renews my weary soul
It refreshes me
It relaxes me
Yes.
Yes, it was worth it.

BEAUTY

Riding through the mountains
On the back of the Harley.
The air is chilled, yet dry.
Thoughts are minimal,
As we wind through Highway 20.
The pines…
The cedars…
The ferns…
Cocooning us as we leave
Nevada County behind.
Lake Tahoe ahead.
A day of beauty.

The journey is as grand
As the destination.
As rocks tower over us.
We are at one with the sky.
The hazy mountains seem surreal.
This is a ride for peace.
A day cloaked in precious beauty
That I am wrapped in.
I embrace the moment,
Feeling the renewal.
If only for that instant,
It is enough.

REST STOP

The rest stop sits high in the Sierra Mountains.
It is my place to stop...to wander...
To take in the mountain's beauty.
I never pass it by without stopping.
It brings me good luck, I've concluded.
Yet, it's more than a place of convenience.
It holds memories of past trips.
Of a distant Pearl Jam Concert...
Of relief from summer heat...
Of sun reflecting off snow.
It's the burst of spring blossoms...
The dramatic colors of fall...
And best of all...icy winter splendor.
A place to hike and explore...
Or build a snowperson and throw snowballs...
To eat our lunch and feed the squirrels.
A place to take pictures...lots of them.
It is my special place to stop—a piney tradition.
Today we roar in and remove our helmets.
Now is the time to enjoy the summer day...
At my special rest stop.

BIRTHDAY RIDE

The sun lights our way.
The asphalt absorbs it.
The wind carries my hair,
Rearranging it like an artist.
There is:
No leather
No windshield
No chill.
It's July on the back of a Harley.
I sit and enjoy the summer day,
While celebrating my day of birth.

EDGE

The edge of the world meets us
As we roar forward.
Greeting my senses
...My soul.
There are no boundaries
...In this place.
Only sound.
Only feelings.
Only nature.
It all reaches out...
Surrounding us with the forest.
As we float by...
Like we're on an escalator.
Each motion touches places
With a freedom that:
Brings peace...
Brings joy...
Brings wonder...
Riding on the edge,
Amongst the pines, firs, and ferns
...On a motorcycle.

RACE

We race through the landscape.
Going towards.
Going past.
Leaving behind.
Yet nowhere we need to be.
We are in the splendor,
Aware of our surroundings.
I could just reach out.
Touch it all...
And breathe it in.
As we dash through it.
Atop our motorcycle,
Racing into the moment.

DOUBLE YELLOW

Gliding down the road
A double yellow line
Separates the directions
While two white lines hold us in
Guiding us on the road
Past, and with, other travelers.
Everyone heading to their own place
Yet, following the rules.
We honor that double yellow line
Hoping to stay safe
In our own artificial place.
But we watch for that one person.
The one who dares to cross
In their hurry to get somewhere
In spite of us being here.
That line can't protect us then.
But it's still there.
A warning for those who heed it.
A challenge for those who don't.
Just some yellow paint
With so much meaning behind it
Trying to keep us all safe.

WRITE

I write in the winds
As they tug at the pages.
I put words on the tan paper
In my little blue journal.
The sun bears down on me,
The sounds are soothing,
I take in all I see,
In the forest and around me.
On the back of a Harley,
On my husband's backbones...
I write.

HEADING

Heading down the highway
Back to where I live.
We wind down the mountain
Into our quaint little town.
Off to my left in between tall pines,
Across the forest I get a glimpse.
There's a mountain with two peaks.
This is my mountain.
It is where I live.
The place I call home.
We fly down the pavement
To where my heart resides...
My soul rejuvenates...
My body rests.
Filled with anticipation heading home.

A PROMISE

Green brims with yellow, orange, pink, and purple.
Butterflies sunning as we fly through the landscape
We are exposed to the beauty on our ride.
Where nature becomes a place of glory.
We ride on toward the adventure...
That only a spring day can promise.

ROAR

The roar of the engine washes away silence.
The winds carelessly cleanse my sins.
My eyes can only absorb so much.
I close them to the moist green beauty.
Vibrant flowers are an explosion of life.
A gust pounds against my skin.
The taste of spring soothes my heart
But it's my soul that reaches out
Only it is able to take it all in—
Then, only then, am I completed in bliss.

THRUST

We are thrust forward into the future,
Riding a magical mechanical being.
Its roar is loud, but its hearing is pure.
Each moment becomes a fond memory,
That I carefully store away.
I enjoy each thrust of my journey
On my spring ride on the back of the Harley.

SUGAR PINES

Your greenery reaches straight out—toward me.
Your branches laden with—large cones.
Your seeds fill the air—like gentle butterflies.
You tower above us all—a sentry.
Seeing all there is to see—for miles.
You stretch to the sun—for warmth.
Enjoying a beautiful fall day—before winter.
The sugar pines stand tall—in splendor.

MOTORCYCLE

The mountains surround us:
Rocks, trees, and dirt.
We keep climbing
On our motorized horse.
We pause only once,
Capturing all that is to be seen.
As we slide back into the world,
Gifted to us on our motorcycle.

DREAM

The diesel-scented air
Rushes past me...
Blowing away my cares.
The sun warm on my skin,
As the roar buries my thoughts.
The sky blue and clear.
The road is smooth
As we are guided
Up into the mountains.
Away from it all
The world submerges us
In the motorcycle's dream.

HUMAN-MADE HORSE

The tree-dotted granite fills my eyes.
Nothing is separate from the landscape—
On a motorcycle.
We fly close enough to touch,
As the landscape grasps at us.
On our human-made horse,
I am closer to nature at this moment.
Thanks to technology and a whim.

BEAUTY

The beauty of the mountains
Warms my heart and chills my hands.
The tall pines reach out to me
Offering the breath of life that fills me.
The smaller trees spill yellow and red.
They're planted firmly in granite rocks.
It is in all directions that my eyes take me.
Nature is swaddling my soul.
It's like a careful mother of fauna.
In this beauty is where I gladly roam.

A RIDE

The granite and trees…
Are our walls.
The clear blue sky…
Our ceiling.
The ground is our…
Moving support.
The river our map…
Our direction.
The engine's roar…
Announcing our presence.
Freedom envelopes us…
As splendor on our ride.

LIKE A BIRD

The green mountains reach up to the blue sky.
We glide like hawks as the wind tugs my hair.
My eyes absorb my surroundings...
The beauty...The rumble of the engine.
The screech cuts through the air's silence.
As we make our descent toward the valley.
We loudly continue to glide like a bird.

MOMENTS

Moments of splendor on the back of a motorcycle
Are impolitely interrupted by roadwork.
We bake in the sun that our black leather absorbs.
Motorcycle off—we sit and wait.
We are silent in the line of cars.
Watching for signs of movement ahead,
When a single butterfly attracts our attention.
It is the flutter within the delay.
Soaring from one side of the road to the other,
It's in a final autumn quest.
The flowers are giving forth their final blooms.
This butterfly rests on a late-budding plant.
My husband and I smile at each other.
Then the enchantment quickly dissipates
When the first car passes us...then another.
Soon, our direction will be moving.
The motorcycle roars into life,
As the butterfly makes one last trip past us.
Our time with this elegant being is gone.
As the quiet fades into the past we're on our way.
But, the memory of the white and orange butterfly
Stays with us on our journey...
As moments of splendor never really end.

OPEN

I'm open to the world
Seated on the back of a Harley.
Winds free me...nature welcomes me.
Trees blanket me in their beauty.
The sun warms my exposed skin—
As it rules the sky.
But there is a change bursting through.
Fall is making its presence known.
Red, yellow, and orange flowing through.
Before I move on it becomes a part of me.
I'm exposed to change while comfort perched,
On the back of the bike, open to the world.

THE RIVER AND THE MOTORCYCLE

The river sits below the road
And we sit on our motorcycle.
We mimic the river's roaring passage
As it surges over the boulders and rocks.
Our tires roll over the pavement,
Leaving behind the growl of the engine.
Both going somewhere, but for now...
We are headed in the same direction.
One in a riverbed, one on a road.
Both moving forward...
Both taking a journey...
Both synchronized...
The river and the motorcycle.

PERCHED

I sit perched on the back of a Harley.
Each corner gently sways me.
Above the black asphalt is the open blue sky.
This is my crown that fills me with life and beauty.
The pines and cedars are guarding my experience.
A bridge approaches.
We majestically cross the mighty Yuba River.
Through the air, on the road, over the water:
We are regally balanced in this world.
The ceremony is accompanied by loud pipes.
As we move forward in our own world.
Where in this moment—
We're perched on a gas throne.

THE RIDE

The river flows in beauty
Rushes in the opposite direction
That our journey is taking us.
The sweet smells surround.
We ride above this waterway—
As witnesses on our motorized freedom.
The water dashes down its rocky route.
The sun reflects the stony bottom.
Campers stake their tents next to it.
Trees remind me of walls of a house.
We are a most welcomed guest—
On our motorcycle ride.

Seasons of a Soul

THE EMOTIONS
Darkness and Light

YOUR WORDS

You feel so powerful and in control.
A keyboard.
Your words.
No consequences.

You don't see the pain.
Cruel talk.
Shoulders slumping.
Souls crushed.

You're educating that person.
Never seen.
Haven't met.
Tears flowing.

You are only spreading your truth.
Its reality.
Their pain.
No dilemma.

They took it wrong and are too sensitive.
Toughen up.
Buckle down.
Who cares.

Wait, you were only trying to be funny?
No laughter.
No smiles.
Only frowns.

What if someone said that to you?
Suffer hurt.
Experience pain.
Feel low.

It's not effective, it's cruel.
Keep writing.
Attack more.
Be alone.

It's your choice to spread negativity over caring.
Give support.
Show love.
Be happy.

BURDEN

You burden me with your words.
They are heavy and persistent.
Coming in huge waves like a tsunami,
Triggered by endless thoughts with no end in sight.
They reach out to everyone around them.
Eyes glaze, shoulders droop, and sighs weigh the air.
You don't notice the response and keep coming at us.
One tale after another of how they did you wrong.
It's the same story over and over.
Yet, you're always surprised they did this—said that.
I silently reflect, that is how they are.
As your words pour over me, I feel like I'm drowning.
I'm your captive audience until, you finally pause.
I respond hoping you hear me this time, but you don't.
You reject my life preserver and I can do no more.
I lovingly smile and gently detach, that is all I have to offer.
I wish you well and leave in blissful silence.

LOVE AND FEAR

Some relationships are based on love, others fear.
I've seen both. One is comfortable and kind.
One is insecure and afraid, both can fall into anger.
Yet, love doesn't stay there long, and fear thrives on it.
Love holds you up, while fear weighs you down.
I found love and it's my foundation and comfort.
Love lingers in passion, prosperity, and peace.
Love has no filter and brings clarity and focus.
It is a beautiful place full of color, texture, and warmth.
Love blooms, while fear wilts the very same flower.
Fear finds passion, its filtered glimpse is quick and hot.
It leaves a scar like a burn that's disturbing and shadowed.
Fear holds people together in misery that's heavy and dark.
It doesn't see the light peeking in darkness, love is living in the light.
Love tries to share it, but fear fights it while mocking.
Jealousy rules fears actions and love extends an open invitation.
Fear doesn't accept. Love sighs gently and moves on.
It hopes fear will see that glimmer of hope right in front of it.
The warm, bright sun offering the purest state of being—love.

FEAR AND LOVE

Fear and hate or love and kindness
Two different places to live and visit.
We choose which place to reside.
We create the foundation with fear or love.
Then, we put up walls to protect our stillness
We fill our house with either fear or love
A cold, hard stool to worry upon,
Or a beautiful warm couch to comfort us.
Sometimes we decorate with both.
But one side finally consumes the other.
Next, we bring others into our lives.
They're offered fear: control, jealousy, and indifference.
The other choice is love: joy, freedom, and patience.

Sometimes, we paint in colors of disapproval,
Until we redecorate in lessons and love.
Mistakes become beauty and fear dissipates into love
Yet, some houses are hauntingly hateful.
Fear shops in other's anger and judgment rules.
Then they look for more searching for sales.
Fifty percent off hate. They stock up and head home.
They never find what they are really looking for.
Love isn't a thing and can't be bought.
It comes from the heart, soul, and above.
It's the only thing that is lasting and a foundation to build on,
Fear leaves you empty, but love will fill your life with joy.
It's your choice fear and hate or love and kindness.

FOUND

I found it and I'm lucky.
I know.
Each day it touches my soul.
I smile.
I forget to express it.
I recognize.
Because it's so much a part of me.
I love.
I go into the world each day.
I live.
Sometimes I see love and happiness.
I grin.
Sometimes I see fear and pain.
I cry.
I attempt to help those in pain.
I'm rejected.
Each night I go home to love.
I recover.
I rest cradled in love.
I'm grateful.
I pray for all to be found.
I am.

HATE

I feel it coming in waves like a hurricane passing over me.
Blaming all in its path, it leaves destruction in its wake.
Arrogance rains down hard on its devastation,
Damaging all it touches, temporarily dictating moments.
It tries to drive away all love with its fear-filled reality.
But I can survive—ride it out—evacuate until it departs.
Knowing it's my choice how I handle the hurricane of hate,
Because with faith as my foundation…I know…I can rebuild.

LOVE WINS

Love always wins but maybe not at first.
Fear and hate do their best to darken *its* light.
Extinguish *it* in lies and turn everything against *it*.
It's a false reality where love may falter or feel sad.
Although *it* may even wonder why or feel abandoned.
It may almost give up but love ultimately doesn't.
It keeps going each day remembering *its* light.
It trusts what *it* is and moves past fear and anger.
In fact, the love invites fear along, even with *its* contempt.
Love tries to release all negativity using *its* pure light.
Fear, anger, and hate fight the gesture with scorn.
But the finale ends the same—*love* wins.

NO LOVE?

You are what's left when there's no love.
When evil entices the purest form of fear and paranoia
Sickness grasps your gut firmly in rage.
You quickly work to extinguish any remaining love around you
By controlling, lying, and manipulating behind a calm exterior.
People are fooled, and they blindly follow you.
Soon, they become buried under addictions and insecurities.
Darkness consumes them, until they become like you.
Yet it's only a nightmare they're in, a place lacking love.
Love is waiting next to them ready to fill the desolate darkness.
When they let love in their emptiness is healed...
Evil is banished, because it can't live in love's light.

IT'S GONE

It's gone...the anger, the pain...gone.
In its place is a spark...of hope...of love.
Feelings that have been hidden that I couldn't feel
I was lost in darkness and pain—suffocating in anger
I couldn't see my truth, what I was:
My soul...
My heart...
My love...
They came out from behind the clouds
It was a small beam of light at first
But the clouds dissipated, and the blue skies emerged
The sun warmed me, and I saw my life again
Different...but mine
I glanced back as the night faded into the horizon
I prayed for those still in the darkness to be strong
Until their clouds lift and they see the colors of life.

WATCHING

I'm unsure what to feel.
I watch the banter flow back and forth
Like the waves on the ocean's shore.
When I've tried to jump in, the water was cold
And the waves almost knocked me down.
The birds were gone, the sand littered with dead-fish
Everything departed or dying.
The oily water covers the hidden riptide.
It wasn't safe, so I sit perched on a hill high above.
Below is a place I used to love, now it's deserted.
While I'm protected from the pandemonium below
The struggle spills out and almost reaches me.
But for now, I'm safe—watching.

PIECES

You are always safe here I try to reassure.
Your eyes flicker with hope for a brief moment,
But suspicion quickly replaces that hope
I know your trust is hard to come by.
Yours has been shattered into many pieces.
I cannot find all those pieces—yet.
I won't give up though until I return them to you.
I'll find a way to relight the hope in your youthful eyes.
Bit by bit I will search with as much help as I can find.
It's not going to be easy, but that doesn't stop me.
Others may give up—I won't.
Because I know once you are safe and loved
Some day...some day...the light will shine again.
All your pieces will be put back together.
And all of you can be whole once again.

NOTHING

Their words fall empty, although they put the right words together.
They should make sense, but they don't. Their body is tense.
They're waving their hands sporadically while waiting for a response.
I have none.
Their breath is fast and erratic as they touch my arm.
I feel nothing.
I search for logic and reason while their words fall around me.
They pause.
I need to reply. "Maybe it was just…" I lamely start.
They quickly jump in with another tangled denial.
"Well, we'll figure this out…" I hear myself say.
That seems to satisfy them, yet inside I still feel nothing.

SILENCE

It is fleeting in that moment.
In between events it waits.
Motionless
Moving
Magnetic—
It is calling you.
Unheard
Unnoticed
Untethered
Until time fades into darkness.
The exact instant you close your eyes.
It's still there waiting—Silence.

MY SOUL

My soul encompasses day and night simultaneously.
My step is light and heavy with joy and burden.
My eyes absorb all the flawed beauty that surrounds me.
The rose's purity blankets the stench of today's waste.
The wind delicately carries conflicting confessions.
Soft humming is the background for the bee's labor,
While the leaves make their final journey to the earth.
A lone voice in the distance carries a surfacing rage.
It's like a volcano erupting into the blue brightness.
The sun peeks out shedding light on this fury.
Roadkill lays next to the blooming lilies.
Good and bad surround me and are in me.
Only my soul can make the right choice—if I let it.

WELCOME TO THE WORLD

Most babies come into the world
With eyes that embrace everything
With ears that welcome all the words
With arms waiting to hug.
Their hearts are overflowing with love.
Babies show the world what is possible…
Of things that can't be seen, only felt.
Yet, bit by bit, babies turn into adults.
They forget all the blessings they came with.
Sometimes, from good intentions, sometimes not.
Their hearts wither away.
Their eyes close to beauty.
Their ears filter the words through fear.
Until one day this is what they expect.
The baby is gone, along with limitless love.
The adult overflows with fear, hurt, and anger.
Until the words passing their lips are guarded.
Their arms push away now—not reaching out.
All that innocence is lost or buried.
Somewhere it waits to be embraced again.
To be brave
To reach out
To speak its truth.
Yet adults watch apprehensively while worrying.
Why aren't they happy they ask?
They search for it

They pay for it
They bring it home.
Yet, it isn't what they're looking for.
But if they stop looking, they might find it.
Tucked safely away where it always been—inside.
Same as the day they were welcomed into the world
If only they can let go of their learned fears
They can find the truth that babies know
That love is the only true state to be.

BRAVE

It was a brave thing you did doing what scared you.
Yes, very brave. Yet, you held back.
You hid even though you were there.
Your lips smiled as the words crossed them.
Your eyes were empty, shoulders tense,
Your mind vacant but you were filled with words.
Truth was trapped in your throat.
Muscles tight...
Breath shallow...
Heart racing...
Sweat covering your body...
You knew you were being brave,
Stepping onto the battlefield with your sword.
But when the time came you only watched
From behind a tree where no one could hurt you.
You knew your fears were controlling you.
They came from a past long gone.
Yet, it was still brave to show up.
That wasn't enough for you this time.
There was more to give, say, and do.
You look around—it is only you now.
It's time you assure yourself...and it is.
You bravely advance leaving your past behind.
Leaving your fear behind.
Leaving your scars behind.
You embrace what seemed like a battlefield
Now it is only a field of your departed fears.
No blood flows on this field, only love.
With the fears gone, you bravely follow the love.

FALL

You fall.
You are in a strange place with strangers,
Depending on their kindness to hold you up.
Then you're laid down in comfort and safety.
They feed you...
Cover you...
Comfort you...
They make sure you are okay.
Even though you didn't know them
And they didn't know you, it didn't matter.
Because you fell and they helped you.
It is all any of us can do,
On either side—to help or be helped.
When the moment arises, do the right thing.
Life really is that simple during a fall.

DECIDE

Life becomes overwhelming, you can't take anymore
But you can and you do,
While floating in a pool of demands.
Distress...
Doubt...
Disappointment...
Depression.
It's heavy and hard, but there's more to life:
Dreams...
Desires...
Dazzling...
Delight.
Your choice which you choose
To live and love your existence
Deem...
Decide...
Develop.
Accept how you feel in any moment,
But only you can decide on your divine truth.

NOTHING

There is nothing and something simultaneously.
It is confusing, yet perfectly comprehensible.
It is black and white...
Night and day...
Cold and hot...
Sad and happy...
Sour and sweet...
Unknown and recognized.
All happening at the same time.
It is what we choose or don't.
Ours to except or not.
But it is nothing to compare.
And nothing to end up being.
Yet nothing is where you start.

NOW

I am alone.
Yet the voices from my past sit with me.
They can haunt me—or comfort me.
I push them all away with intention
I'm looking for that peace I hear about.
I quiet my past to move toward my future,
While I sit firmly in my now.
I wait.
At times I feel that joy and love.
I realize that it had always been there.
I was too busy listening to my past,
While planning my future—I didn't notice.
My now exists without:
My acknowledgment...
My permission...
Or belief...
As I sit alone, I can finally connect it all.
I see and I am. That is all there is in my now.

SHADOW

It is there right behind you.
Watching...
Waiting...
Wary.
It's your shadow and part of your life.
It sees all you do and makes no comment.
Its companionship is unnoticed yet constant.
You keep going unaware of its presence
Yet there it is—right behind you.

SILENCE

It is an unusual soundless silence.
I stand in a dark vacuum.
Empty yet full, as the air thickens.
The ground is solid and the night warm.
But there is no noise.
No crickets...
No wind...
No dogs barking...
No cars driving...
No TVs blaring...
No distant trains.
It's unnerving standing there in the inky night.
The dogs join me, subdued as they water the landscape.
In that moment it is only us, then it is gone.
I quickly forget the nothingness
Where the darkness briefly consumed me.
I shiver, petting the dogs and head inside.
I'm safe from the sinister silence—for now.

SLEEP

It comes every night, unless it doesn't.
You fall into a quick slumber or toss and turn.
Replaying your entire day, or entire life.
You hear sounds and turn on a nightlight.
You check the doors and windows—locked.
You toss and turn more.
You remember something you needed to do.
You look at the clock—it mocks you.
You try deep breaths being grateful,
But the worry creeps back in.
You wish it was a night you fell into sleep,
Waking up ready to tackle your worries.
But this isn't one of those nights,
As the darkness fades to light.
Your alarm goes off right after you—fall asleep.
Your day begins whether you slept or not.
It doesn't matter until sleep comes again…or doesn't.

INNOCENCE

You are open and kind.
Your mind embraces everything.
You judge no one.
You wonder about the world.
You have a joy in everything you do.
There is still a trust that…
Everything will be all right.
There is a hope that people…
Will always do the right thing.
There is a faith it will work out.
There's a pureness in you an innocent child.
That innocence that hasn't been formed…
Into a thinking adult, a logical being.
That realistic fearful person.
Where paranoia and fear rule.
Where judgment and anger are normal.
Where no child exists…
Under all the grown-up responsibilities.
The pressure of it all pushes out…
The last of that youthful innocence.
Leaving a place where nothing ever works out.
There is no joy, and other people…
Are only out to get you.
May we nurture this child into adulthood.
May the child's faith spread into society…
And fill all the cracks of adulthood.
Making this a world of innocence…
Filled with joy and love once again.

PEACE

We all look for peace.
Sometimes we find it, other times we don't.
It is not far though can be deeply buried
Under work and obligations,
Under illness and noise.
It's quiet, gentle, and patient.
Loving and kind it awaits our attention.
It doesn't scream to be noticed.
That's why we forget it's there.
But it is, and it's not going anywhere.
Peace is content where it is—it always is
It makes you smile when you think about it.
In that moment you know it—and it knows you.
And that is the place you wish to live forever.
But your life calls you and you answer.
You forget to invite your new friend with you.
But peace isn't mad, it just waits until next time.
When you remember it's there...
Waiting for you...just waiting peacefully.

MATTERS

You were there a really long time.
You know that, though.
You used to like it, now you don't.
In fact, you hate it.
There was a time when you didn't want to live—
Yet, you've stayed way past that point
Waiting for what I'm not sure.
Finally, you make a move to a new place.
A space to be happy—perhaps.
It will be different and difficult to arrive at.
Change never is easy, but you might fit in.
You might be happy again in this place.
As you take that first step forward,
Leaving that long time in your past.
You knew it well, but it stripped you away.
Bit by bit until you were a shell.
Yes, it may have been a long time,
But you still have more time ahead.
That will be a long time, too.
In a place to be happy,
Where everything will be different.
That is all that matters.
In all of time—that is all that matters.

I GET MAD

Yes, I admit I get mad.
It eats away at me...
Slowly digesting my soul.
It would finish the job if I let it,
But I won't let it—I have to live my life.
Being mad takes life away from me.
Finally, I let go and send prayers out.
I hope they find happiness of their own.
When they let go of their side of their anger.
So they won't live in their madness.
I send them love...it's all I can do.
With a breath and a smile I move on.
Cutting the ties of hate once and for all,
Because I have no time to be mad.
When all that is important in life is—love.

SADNESS

It is deep, dark, and anchors me to its agony.
Its hands tighten on my throat and its eyes pierce my soul.
Its mouth extracting my lifeforce, while I try to escape.
I've become a fugitive trying to flee a painful process of panic.
Over the memories…
Over the future…
Over the shame.
It scorches me as I silently struggle to breathe.
I'm weighed down by its oppressive grief.
This sadness washes over me like a tsunami's wave.
It consumes me with its rage washing over me.
I cling to the nearest tree, but I can't hold on.
It rips me away drowning me in its discomfort.
My fight disappears as I sink into the darkness.
"No!" I cry as it embraces me in heavy desolation.
Every moment…mistakes…misunderstanding.
I'm disheartened as a hand reaches for me.
I pull away. *I can't*—I tell myself.
I can't. *Let go*…I hear. *Let go*…I do.
At first, I am swallowed in the obscurity.
I swirl thinking that shadows had tricked me,
But my fight had been restored, rushing through me.
It's still okay, it says. Now I can stand.
I bravely walk out of the darkness, boldly into safety.
I collapse into the protection of the promise.
Sadness rules only for the moment, not forever.

I accept that knowing it's the only way there is.
I went with the sadness' surge, accepting it.
It rushed past me and left me covered in mud—but alive
Because hope reached out to me and I took its hand.
I am safe for now even in the darkness...I always was.

SIMPLY GONE

Gone is that elusive past, yet it's right here next to me.
It keeps me awake full of faults and fears,
While it tries to inject me with its venom and guilt.
I shudder in the repulsion of a scenario of my own creation.
It may be over, but it still exists inside of me.
Like a secret hoarder holding on to an old discarded shirt.
The closet in my mind is full of things I don't need.
There's no room for anything new behind this closed door.
Hidden behind a face is a place where pain can't be seen.
You're shown a smile, while my heart is breaking.
I push that pain away hopefully for the last time.
I know this is my personal penance I've long outgrown.
It's filled me until there is no room for anything else.
It's time to let go of the things I've collected.
Leaving room for my heart to shine through my smile.
Then my peace will be complete within my soul.
I can move forward in my future leaving all that unused
   baggage.
I'll be focused on the present because I've already lived the past.
It is simply gone.

WAKE UP

Wake up and see what's right in front of you.
Listen to what is being said and don't numb yourself.
It's okay to be alone…to sit quietly, peacefully, and breathe.
Observe your feelings…what is right and wrong.
Don't let the fears controlling you shut them out.
Yes, take that deep breath. You're safe and loved.
Right, that's it…breathe…No, don't do that.
Come back…focus and relax. No, you aren't bored.
You're afraid. Eyes glaze over with a hand on the TV remote.
Bad news quickly pours in and your awareness shuts down.
Next, adrenaline kicks in feeding your addiction to chaos.
You've been lost for the moment, but the quiet is there.
In the quiet is the reason that will appear in your serenity.
You will find me there…waiting for you to wake up.

PERFECTION

They sit in a pink vase in stagnant water on the dresser.
It's meant to make you feel better—it has.
The yellow roses give life to the room in their death.
Their sweet aroma covers the illness with their delicate beauty.
They take away the darkness with their perfection.
In a joyless world they give everything, then are thrown away.
If the flowers are lucky their image stays with us in a picture.
Finally, they begin to wilt, their usefulness gone—
They meet their expected end and are disposed of.
The pink vase now sits empty in a dark cabinet,
Waiting for its next appearance to hold more perfection.
In a world fill with much imperfection they're a bearer of hope.

EVIL AND THE ENABLER

They are inside me, but no one knows during the day.
I forget about them sometimes until I'm rudely reminded,
In the darkness of the night making their presence known.
Heavy, controlling and demanding my attention.
There to point out all the things I've done wrong—
Since the day I was born.
My heart races as my mind spins out of control,
Stomach clenched removing any doubt.
Racing through the night like an asteroid in my mind,
Evil has crashed into my deepest fears and sins.
It was greeted graciously by an enabling host.
The host fed it slowly, as each mouthful poisoned my soul.
Embedded deeply at the crash site I've found no cure…or
 escape.
Uninvited chaos, I've attempted to evict them: enabler and evil.
But they dug in deeper. One seems to feed off the other now.
I watch for them in the light of day, but darkness is when they
 come.
Sometimes they almost win feeding off me, until I send them
 back.
As soon as they're banished, my stomach settles…my mind
 calms.
Then my eyes shut tightly in a fitful sleep, ending one of those
 nights,
When darkness encourages evil and its enabler to emerge from
 inside.

Covering all the lights, except for the nightlight I always leave burning.
Sometimes I have a hard time finding that glow, but it's always there.
Then, I'm not scared anymore after finding my safe place in the darkness,
And evil and its enabler have been pushed back by my light—until next time.

THE SHOE

I'm figuring out why I keep repeating the same issue over and over,
Like walking by a shoe in the middle of the room, tripping over it daily,
But not moving it or even taking another route so I don't fall over that shoe.
Then it became guilt for me, always been there, while I kept tripping on it.
You'd never know, though, no one sees me fall, I pretend to be quite graceful,
I'm not, although no one sees my bruises, which makes it all okay.
Except now at life's insistence, I need a new path around the old shoe.
A shoe bought by people I didn't want to be like.
They polished it, bronzed it, and placed it on display for me.
I watched others put their shoes away in their closets.
Mine stayed as a constant reminder of my failure.
Finally, today I realized I could pick it up and put it in my closet.
It didn't even have to be neat, just safe.
Now, I can walk safely across the floor without falling.
For the first time in my life no guilt to trip on.
The change came inside of me when the shoe found its home.
I am free and someday I will throw this shoe away…someday.

THE WAIT

The clock moves forward—moody in the silence
The black leather chair supports my weight
People pass through offering help I don't need
The dull brown rugs and orange accent hold me up
The phone silent...
The desk unmanned....
The other chairs empty...
A pain in my chest...
My stomach clenched in worry...
The air is heavy with sadness and pain.
It is a world filled with fake smiles
Help is applied away from watchful loving eyes
I write, I worry, as I wait...only wait.

SMILE

Your smile lights up the room
Your anger sucks it back into darkness
All the words being said about you
Maybe they are true...yet...
I believe in you still
I will hold you up
I will fight for you
I see your soul
Under all that behavior
I still see you, even though
Life spins out of control
I take a deep breath
And focus on your smile
Just your soul's smile.

CAMERA

Our lives come down to a camera sitting perched on our house.
It watches, waiting to capture someone behaving badly.
It watches who comes and goes for viewing later if needed.
It shows us the view when the dogs bark with false comfort.
We have come down to this state of no trust or safety.
Privacy gone in exchange for security that watches and waits.
We hope that our fears are never recorded on our camera.

RIGHT/WRONG

Who is right, who is wrong?
Is it that simple of a question?
Do actions speak louder than words?
Do they only offer reflection?
Do they bring any clarity?
Yet, the answer is there, it doesn't matter,
Who was right and who was wrong.
Right or wrong: only the solution matters.

LOSS AND GAIN

My losses and gains over the years have been extreme.
Sometimes I ride high thinking nothing would touch me,
All was right in my world and I was invincible.
Later, a heavy loss would wipe that all away.
I thought I'd linger in the immensity of that loss for eternity
Thinking nothing would change…it would, though.
Gains would change the gloom.
I would grasp at the good times with my entire being.
Each moment fully lived not worrying what was to come.
Unfortunately, it always came when I least expected it.
In ways I couldn't imagine on a bright sunny day came a storm.
Sometimes the storm would pass immediately or sit upon me.
I would have no shelter as the rains pelt down.
At times I was left battered and bruised in my time of loss
Darkness would set in, heaviness weighed me down.
Yet, each moment I drew a new breath and my heart kept beating.
That small moment told me I wasn't done. I was still here.
No matter—how grim things looked.
No matter—I had any answers.
No matter—I was breathing and waiting.
Soon the clouds began to part, rain stopped, and the sun appeared.
An unexpected gift finally found its way to me and I gladly accepted.

Not worried about the next storm…maybe I should have been.
Maybe I should have prepared, but for right now I enjoyed my gain.
I gladly embraced my good fortune until the next loss—I live in my gain.

SAME

We all need each other, although we may not know it.
We fight and argue, while ending up no one was right.
Our goals are the same, but our approach different.
This flares our anger and listening stops.
The needs never leave and hide under the pain.
Sadness lingers until that day, we pause and notice.
Our anger is gone, and confusion has replaced it.
We walk through the dawn of our enemy.
We end up in the same place by a different path.
What happened, we wonder, with ideas so unalike?
Our transportation wasn't the same, but our needs were.
Today society has the same needs, but varied approaches.
I wonder and wait for that moment when the whole world
Walks into the same room and through the same door
Meeting with the same goal...this time with love in our hearts.

THE EMOTIONS
Those Feelings

WHIRLWIND

It entered my life like a storm…
Blowing everything familiar away from me.
I clung to the numbness it left behind.
It holds me above the weight of evil
That tries to drown me in its darkness.
I gasp to fill my lungs in this whirlwind
That swirls life around me hitting me with debris.
I've stopped ducking the pain, coming to expect it.
My normal life is ripped away from me, cruelly.
My comforts—gone
My emotions—grim
My distrust—growing
I swirl in this whirlwind brought to me like a present…
All I can do is survive this whirlwind of illness.

I WORRY

The pain settles in on my left side
I worry
My arm hurts
I worry
My stomach is churning
I worry
I try to shake if off
I worry
I take deep breaths
I worry
I push the pain hoping it will recede—it does
I worry
Fear settles in as I realize it's lessened…
I worry
Could signal a heart attack
I worry
Stress envelopes me in a tight tenseness
I worry
I worry that I worry
Then again, I worry
I shake my pain off, but the worry remains

SEASONS OF MONEY

Money flows into our lives much like the seasons.
There can be an abundance or a scarcity of the greenery.
Things can be growing—or withering on the vine.
It starts in spring as we carefully plant our crops.
They continue to grow under our watchful eye in summer.
Our labors rewarded as we sit around the table celebrating.
But fall also prepares us for the cold winter days ahead
When the chill blankets everything in ice and snow.
While we're mindful of what was stored for winter months ahead,
We're hopeful that spring will return in our seasons of money.

CHANGE

It is changing all around us and it doesn't matter where you live.
Hurricanes, tornados, fires, droughts, or floods...
It will find you because no one is safe from this change.
My own beloved forest is showing signs with the pines dying.
Groves of brown trees litter our view in patches of death.
They feed the underlying fuels for the fires to come and they will.
Droughts stronger...
Hurricanes intense...
Fires deadlier...
Tornadoes massive...
Rains unforgiving...
Floods spreading...
Oceans rising...
Lakes dying...
All is changing.
We have to adapt to it and be ready but aren't.
This is all only a symptom of a world out of control.
A place that we tried to control with so much change.
But we must change now, before it's too late.

FIRE

The word strikes fear if you bravely live in the mountains.
Will a thunderstorm start a blaze?
Will the wind start a new fire?
Will the wall of flames come from humans?
It is something we live with when we live with the trees.
We're no safer than the squirrels or bears—fire doesn't care.
It will rip through trees or a house with no preference.
In its destruction it takes it all—until nothing remains.
Then, when the smoke clears, and life slowly comes back,
The scorched earth recovers in green while animals recoup
So do the humans…so do the humans.
It is rebuilt—but never the same once touched by fire.

WE WAIT

The air is thick with disaster heavy in loss and pain
The sun unable to break through as the winds fuel the flames
Tension fills us all with no breath too deep
As watchful eyes are kept pinned on the horizon
We wait for the warning with bags packed—ready to flee
The air thick with ash from the fires...we wait.

WAIT

Smoke fills the air, as the winds push it toward us
We check the latest update wondering and worrying...
Are our friends and family okay? Are we okay?
A bag is packed...just in case
Animal carriers ready, anxiety fills the hours
Another fire starts, it feels like everything is in flames.
Yet, we are safe...for now.
Praying for rain, our neighbors, and the firefighters
We wait until we hear 100 percent contained
Until the winds have calmed and rain is in the forecast
But for now...the burning fills the air
And all we can do is...wait.

RED FLAG

It is a red flag warning—you hear.
Fire danger high—you've heard it before.
Until you wake up to the announcement:
The schools are closed—due to fires.
You quickly search for information—heart racing.
There are two fires—people evacuating.
Houses, towns, lives…lost.
But there are more fires across the state.
Never has this been seen before on such a scale.
State of emergency—from the night the winds blew
The red flag warnings—that will never be forgotten
By those who survived it, in memory of those who didn't.

IS IT?

So much has happened in the last few weeks—
Hurricanes, tornados, floods, shootings, fires...
Every day has become someone's emergency.
We watch helplessly until it finally arrives at our door.
So much loss, sadness, and pain we try to help.
We survive
We support
We sob
It is overwhelming with each event to process.
State after state falling victim to these occurrences.
Each one leaves us speechless as we helplessly watch.
Some days we can go on, other days it's at our door.
Who to help now, or can we just help ourselves?
Things are changing as each disaster shows us.
It's overwhelming but is it too late? Is it?

DEATH

So many lives lost on the whim of a single person
The pain is unbearable watching it unfold
Lives changed when heroes are born
Grief and sadness fill our hearts
While numbness sets in as the images hit us
"How...why?" we ask.
There is no answer
All we can do is pray in that moment...
Reach out when we see a raised hand.
When so much death...so much pain...
Happens for no reason as we struggle:
To explain, understand, and process.
It is such a senseless act from a stranger
We all live with the mortality imposed on us
And we go forward heavy-hearted
Looking for an answer to a change
That only together we can find it
We must act before it is too late.

LOST

A voice was silenced today after all it had given us.
The songs were left as a gift taking us through:
Joy, understanding, reflections, memories, and pain.
We were guided through all our emotions musically.
Left behind now is a part that will always play on.
We'll remember a song or time weaved into our lives
Given so freely by a mind, guitar, and voice.
It was revealing, raw, and real from our gentle muse.
Although, we grieve the sudden departure…
Of one we knew—but didn't really—yet we understood.
We were understood, too, in those words that told our story.
That can never be taken from us even if you were.
We're grateful for that time and you will always be here
With your wisdom that we cling to now in uncertain times,
As we realize the loss…we break down…for a little while.

PAIN

The pain surges through my body settling into my stomach
There is no position to find relief, no magic potion to save me
Muscles tight and pulling, with stress racking my body.
It is reminding me of my internal pain
How deep inside me it's waiting to be released.
And that one day my pain will finally be gone.
But for now, I wait.

FROM THE BOOK WORLD

EVILDWELS MOVE ON

(based on *This Second Chance* and *The Button*)

Evildwels cannot exist where there is love.
But if there is doubt, fear, and hate they thrive.
They do their best to extinguish any love,
While feeding on the absence of it.
They only win with their own conquests.
Their hunger fed as they discard their victim.
Time is irrelevant to them...
As they search for the rage they need.
It seems to be in abundance for them.
They can pick their cream of the crop
...And then wipe it out.
The battle can be bleak and boundless
...Between good and evil.
But ultimately, it is evil that loses,
When good repairs the broken soul
...It is the stronger of the two.
It may lose the battle but always wins the war,
Then the good in love becomes the happy ending.
Evildwels move on...searching and waiting
For the cruel satisfaction of temporary hosts
In a moment where love is wiped away
Until love re-emerges...and the evildwel moves on.

ABUSE

(inspired by *The Button* and *This Second Chance*)

You've been called stupid and ugly many times—it still hurts.
The words wound you deeper than any hit or punch.
Each slicing remark cuts deep into your soul.
It disfigures you until you are as twisted as the abusers.
No one is there to tell you that you are loved.
That you are beautiful—you are wanted.
Instead, the ignorant utterances hit you faster than a fist.
Each day you have one less tear to cry...
Until one day the tears are finally gone.
Numbness replaces the pain and you're locked safely inside.
Your walls thick and strong until one day...
Someone reaches out to you and you push them away.
They don't leave. Instead they show you kindness.
Slowly you replace the numbness with pain, then healing...
With that caring someone who'll accept your unshed tears.
This is what's been missing in your past: love and acceptance.
They fill the hole left by abuse, leaving only your beauty.

WATCH
(revised from *This Second Chance*)

I watch him and wonder…
Do you love her as much as you love yourself?
Or do you hate her more than you hate yourself?
Your comforts come first…
Your contempt directed at her and never yourself.
Her purpose in life is what she can do for you.
Your purpose is to make her feel she is incapable.
I puzzle…
Why does she keep trying to please you?
Is it out of love or fear? Does she hate herself more than you do?
Is she supposed to respect a person who has none for her?
You show no tenderness
No empathy
No love
No feelings at all
But concern for yourself and it's never your fault—only hers.
Wondering why she stays I try to see her side of this, too.
I know she sees how other relationships go as she admires
  them openly…
When he's not around her face has a sad smile.
She works, is strong, and gives all she has.
Her excuses abound:
He will change if I only…
He's just stressed.
I don't want to be alone.
No one else would want me.

He needs me.
Underneath, he is a good guy.
But his contempt is a bottomless pit of anger.
It feeds his existing darkness and fears.
It almost seems normal at times…until it isn't.
Help or concern is not welcomed
That is until it is—unless it is too late.
Then comes the innocence—a child.
She protects and nurtures it under his watchful eye.
He carefully points out all she does wrong
Without lifting a finger to ease her burdens
He is her judge and jury.
This is her reality and now she feels trapped.
She is trapped in his web spun of lies and hate.
She tries to please and create this illusion of family.
It will get better, she thinks, if they have another child.
I watch helplessly, as my comfort is rejected by his influence.
Right now, it's only words, which bruise her like a fist.
Someday he will cross over from words with an open hand.
Maybe he already has, but that wouldn't be his fault either.
Nothing ever is.
Once I thought she was finally free, but she went back.
Can't help who you love I was told.
But it isn't love. It's hate, insecurity, fear, and above all control.
I hope it isn't too late for her and for all the hers out there.
The ones that feed that bottomless pit of anger they're living with.

It will never be filled, and it will never change what it is.
It is not love.
Silence is empty but heavy on my stomach.
I bite back all the unsaid words, even the ones I've said before.
I quietly wait for you to wake up and come to me. I will help you.
I promise that I don't want to hurt or judge you.
I just want to see you're safe and happy.
To be loved as you are capable of loving.
I wait because you will never be alone.
I wait until you see that.
We all do.
While he is watching your every move…
I am watching him, too.

UNWELCOME GUEST
(from *The Button*)

I feel it when I'm uncomfortable.
It is always there, hiding, waiting.
That shallow breath,
that tight grip—that feeling.

It draws my attention
back to where it came.
A time—
a time when I wasn't so strong.

I was helpless.
I was young.
I'm none of those things now.
Yet it stays.

It's an unwanted guest
that lurks in my body,
that has overstayed
its welcome.

It seems unaware
that it isn't wanted anymore.
So I carefully guide it to the door,
fumbling with the lock.

It clings to the doorway,
hanging onto my past.
Smiling, I gently push it out.
We are both free as I release it.

RELEASE
(based on *The Button*)

I feel it when I'm uncomfortable.
It's there, where it was the last time:
Hiding...
Waiting...
Watching...
That shallow breath...
That tight grip...
That feeling.
It draws my attention to a time,
A time when I wasn't so strong.
I was helpless...
I was young...
I was weak.
I'm none of those things now.
Yet it stays.
An unwanted guest lurking in my body,
That's overstayed its welcome.
It doesn't know it isn't welcome anymore
So, I carefully guide it to the door.

HIDDEN

(Evildwel inspired)

Evil hides among us hidden behind fake smiles.
It lulls you into a false comfort you didn't see coming.
Shiny and beautiful to the eyes...
Soothing and pacifying to the ears...
Soft and gentle as its illusion blankets you.
It strokes your ego with practiced compliments.
Its facade concealed to the unobservant gaze.
Yes, evil is hidden in plain sight among us all.
Because, behind all that deception, darkness awaits.

IF ONLY
(based on *The Button*)

If only you hadn't been born...
The words hit you like a sledgehammer.
But you know it's true...
They would be so much happier without you.
You try to make it up to them...
You are quiet, do well in school, clean for them.
It's never enough...Nothing is.
All you want to do is please them...
But you can't—and you finally stop trying.
You lash out at others...
In the same fashion as was done to you.
You have finally become those words...
Hurtled at you your whole life if only you weren't.
You give up...
You no longer get good grades, clean, or are quiet.
Now you think if only...
If only you hadn't been born and you grant their wish.

TRAPPED

(inspired by *The Button* and *No Fairy Tale*)

I feel her trapped in me...
That scared little girl from so long ago.
I've tried to reassure her...
To embrace her...
To comfort her...
Yet, she still hides...
While trying to protect me.
Scared and in illogical ways that don't.
She doesn't know that though, she's too little.
Too young to understand that I'm okay now.
That I am safe...we are safe.
I keep trying to reach her.
With the hope that someday
She will feel protected
And not try to hold me back...
In her attempt to keep us safe.
That together we can move forward...
Just the two of us...in trust and wonder.

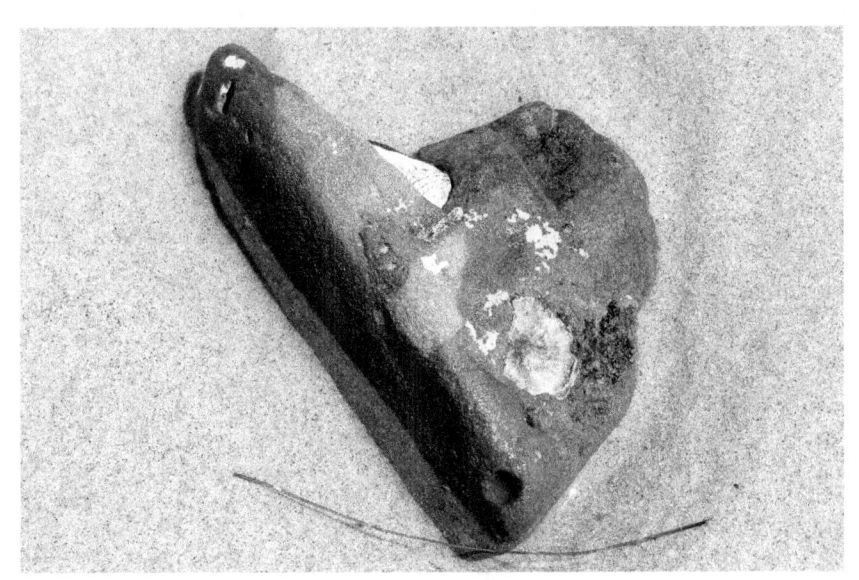

A BIT OF FAMILY

SHOW ME

You showed me where you spend your days.
Each hall had a different story. In between I ask questions.
It made you uncomfortable, but that wasn't my intention.
I want you to learn for yourself, as well as learn things in school.
Our pace quickens, and we have smiles in place. No response.
So, I awkwardly add:
"I only want you to be happy, that is what is most important to me."
You smile.
Maybe you hear me, maybe you don't.
We continue the tour and the moment has passed.
But hopefully I have placed a small seed.
In time it will grow and someday happiness will be your quest.
Someday.
Then you will show me all the things you have learned.

LEAVE

It hurts less each time you leave.
But still you take a piece of me with you.
I think of you in your youth.
A sparkle in your eyes...
Joy in your laughter...
Holding you in my arms...
It all stays with me.
You grew and became.
I was amazed and perplexed.
At times you brought me joy and pain.
I always knew you'd leave,
There was never any doubt.
I felt a bit of pride and sadness,
When you walked to your car.
You're doing what you're supposed to do.
So am I.
You'll always be:
In my heart...
In my mind...
In my prayers.
Every day.
So, leave as you must,
And become what you are.
Distance doesn't mean a thing to me,
Because when you go, a part of me goes with you.
You'll always be my child.

I'll always be your mother.
I know the world deserves you,
And you deserve the world.
I'll go back now into my own world.
Watchful now for that text, *I made it home safely.*
Because mothers never stop worrying.
They never stop being proud.
Or ever stop loving even when their child leaves.

LONG AGO

It was so long ago when I rushed about.
When I hurried, and everything was so important.
So many things had to be done with no time to do them.
Exhaustion was the norm, I fell back into that world.
Only to fill a need with so many things I had to do.
I got tired and I forgot how much work it was.
And I also forgot how much joy it brought, too.
The smiles…
The laughter…
The joy.
Hidden under all the work.
But the work isn't what was important.
It was the questions…
The wonder…
The silliness.
Yet I didn't know that as I felt all the work instead.
Now, I know what is important amongst the chaos.
Too bad we never figure it out when we should,
Which is why grandparents are so important.
They can be the ones who remind everyone
How important the children are while raising them.
Grandparents can raise us up in their memories of the past.
Their insights of what worked and what didn't.
What they did wrong and what they can do now.
Grandparents are far more important today
Than any technology or theory of the moment.
They can offer wisdom not found in a cell phone or browser
Their loving perspective guides the next generation—if we let
  it.

LOVE

I love you and you love me.
We spend so much time together.
We are so happy, this you and I,
Until the world tries to pull us apart.
Attempting to take away what we have,
It uses every dirty trick, yet it never succeeds.
Because we always stop and find each other.
Distance doesn't matter between us, it never has.
Then we cross the bridge between our worlds.
It's a beautiful place by the river fed by a waterfall.
There's a large white gazebo where we meet up.
Here, we take each other's hand in gentle comfort.
My head on your shoulder, we watch the setting sun.
The colors of the landscape matching its purple hues.
We are silent in this splendor, no need for words.
Our feelings are pure and go beyond expression.
It's a place where our love exists eternally.
On the warm sand we sit in a moment of perfection.
No matter what this world throws at us,
We answer it with a love that holds us in bliss.

TOGETHER

These are moments I dream of in our fleeting times together.
Riding through the lush green landscape to see nature's splendor.
Me, in the back seat, smiling broadly in my contentment.
Conversations flow easily, snacks dispersed with celebration.
I reflect on what holds us together. It's not our name or gene pool.
It is more. It's deeper. It's the laughter and shared experiences.
It's trust and love all blended in place, while holding each other up.
Here, we find new wonders together in our brief stops along the way.
Gazing upon the ocean, sitting in the sand where the water meets land
We walk carefully avoiding jellyfish littering the shoreline.
But we are happy as smiles dominate, while the sun warms our skin.
The sea's roar calls us to stay and the salt permeates our souls.
Peacefully gazing at the ocean, I know it heals in ways unrealized.
I breathe in the salty therapy knowing our time together is so brief.
Soon it will be time to part ways and go back to our daily lives.
But we're together for this instant that will go on forever.
It's carefully placed in my memories, where my dreams come true.
Together…even distance doesn't keep us apart.
Together…is where our souls remain.
Together…always in these moments.

HOLIDAYS AND VACATIONS

CHRISTMAS

Once a year it comes.
Bearing gifts, feasts, and good will.
We open our hearts a little more.
Our smiles are hurried, but more genuine.
Pines and fir trees scent the air...
Perched behind the ornaments and decorations.
Our waistlines expand...
As we are plied with cookies and treats.
Cards carefully delivered...
Songs put an extra bounce in our step.

Images of a perfect day fills our thoughts.
We hear from friends far away.
We remember people from our past.
We enjoy the lights, Santa, and maybe snow.
It is a time our hearts remember our inner child.
Each hug more meaningful...
Each memory more important...
Each moment a present....
When our blessings are magnified, because it's Christmas.

WEEK BEFORE CHRISTMAS

It is a week before Christmas
And all through the yard
The cats are running with abandon
Chasing bugs moving like lard.

While the bees found no flowers
The blue sky fills my eyes
My skin absorbs the sun
As I sit peacefully after sunrise.

The lights around my door
Blink red, green, yellow, and blue
Reminding me it's Christmas
Not April, May, or even June, too.

The oak trees are bare
Leaves still litter the landscape
It is a silent warm day
No birdsongs to escape.

I enjoy this warmth and beauty
And I happily embrace whatever is given
Yet I long for the cold days of past
Knowing during the holidays it will be forgiven

Because it's more than weather or wildlife
It is a feeling of love
Sitting on my deck on a warm winter day
I feel Christmas coming from above.

STOCKINGS

The stockings lay unhung.
Christmas is a few days away.
My heart is heavy with things left unsaid.
Of people gone...until we are reunited.
I know it is a time for miracles.
I know even if I can't see them...
They are still with me.
So, I will get up Christmas morning,
With the joy of the day filling my heart.
The miracle will be inside of me.
Even if a stocking remains empty this year...
It is still filled with love.

SILENCE

The day is silent, full of wonder and awe
As Christmas approaches with a hurrah.
There are things to do and places to be
Yet, in this moment the spirit fills me
Joy and wonder abound in the blue skies
And pine trees green without a storm's surprise
No white landscape covering the woodland
A flash of peace where I've the upper hand
In amazement of the silence of this day
Until it all just casually slips away.

HOLIDAY

It is a holiday, you know.
I sit alone—in peace.
I rock slowly in my swinging chair.
It's a gift lovingly given to me a long time ago,
By someone who is still working.

I could be working but choose not to.
Other people are camping
Some hurry to their next event.
The air is heavy with BBQ,
As the birds sit in their nests singing.

The squirrels are caring for their new brood.
The bees hum from flower to flower.
The cats carefully watch them.
I rock in tune to this moment.
Alone—but not lonely.

On this holiday, I have paused
Taking it all in, chores set aside
Work can wait—
But, this moment cannot
As introspective silence relaxes my body.

I'm filled with healing and wonder
All this beauty is always there,
Outside—
Away from my desk,
From my computer.

This holiday I stepped into it
Alone and reverent
In the beauty of nature
Something I could never create—
Only admire.

I inhale it all in
Reflect—
Meditate—
Before the moment is lost,
In the noise of the holiday.

EXPLORE

We set out ready to explore:
See new sights, find new things,
To be amazed and wowed.
In air-conditioned comfort,
Water bottle in tow.
Snacks on the back seat.
Sunscreen applied, map in hand
Full of wonder.
It's recorded with pictures and videos.
For others to see we went sightseeing.
All from the luxury of rented wheels.
We explore!

PACKED AWAY

We wait all year for this moment.
Carefully we apply sunscreen.
Hat, towel, and sunglasses in place,
As we slip onto a lounge with drink in hand.
It's our seven days and nights in paradise.
This moment slips away too quickly.
Soon it is time to pack it all away,
Handing your luggage and moments to the past.
Then, you're flying back to your life.
Yet—a small part of that tropical beauty,
You bury deep inside—until next time.

BEING

Why do people try so hard to have fun?
They plan, anticipate, and prepare for the vacation.
Huddled around the pool they plot the next event.
Washing down reality with relaxing juice,
They're ready for the next exciting thing.
Yet who are they impressing if they do this...
As they check off each item from their internet must-dos?
Then they record it all as proof of completion.
This ends up sitting like a trophy on a shelf
Where it collects dust in a display of good times.
But there are a few who know what vacation is.
They lay dozing in the sun, or quietly reading a book.
They could be strolling on the beach, or swimming in the sea.
They might be sitting on a lounge chair watching people rush
  about.
These few know it's a special place to renew and refresh.
A time to find themselves, even when they weren't lost.
This period is spent healing the inside and outside.
These are the people who will explore with wonder
Not trying to have fun to show others.
They aren't trying at all—they are simply being.

VACATION

I predict, plan, prepare then pack.
Lists checked off, suitcases full and locked.
The day has come, and I set off exhausted.
Dragging myself through each hurtle of the trip.
The destination is as expected—beautiful.
I quickly set out to see as much as possible.
My time is limited and my pace tougher than work.
Each night I fall into an exhausted sleep,
Only to be woken up by a selfish, loud neighbor.
Pillow pressed to my ears, my sleep is gone.
I eat breakfast, planning my day.
Then, I suddenly wonder what happened…
To sitting and reading—to just existing?
I tried it for a day, like a child, I found a simple joy.
Finally, I have discovered my actual holiday
Sitting on my lounge reading and napping.
I peacefully watch the clouds float by.
I'm reminded of my summer's past.
A swim or ice cream with nothing to see or do.
I smile, lay back, and enjoy—my real vacation!

SUN

Sunscreen-covered bodies recline in the sun.
Others float in the pool with passing chatter.
The wind whips the towels and tips an umbrella.
Righted, the disturbance is removed.
The people go back to worshipping the sun,
Glowing in shades of brown, pink, and red.
Proof they had fun in the sun on their tropical vacation.

ISLET

I sit above the pool on my chaise lounge relaxing.
Paradise submerges me as the waves caress the shore.
The gentle tropical breeze keeps me content.
My water bottle is next to me hydrating my soul.
I have a moment where there is nothing to do.
Nothing to say and nowhere to be.
It is a scarce situation for me but welcomed.
I have found my twinkling of peace.
My gaze wanders over to the pool.
So many people busy filling their hours.
My ears ingest their high social bragging
It is loud and coarse in my delicate state.
While they speak of having fun…
Their bodies are tense and alert.
Strange, I think in passing, and tune it out.
I have found my serenity within
My mind is calm and my body comfortable
I'm on my own islet on a tropical island.

CLOUDS

On top of the clouds
I float in a metal bird.
The sea is speckled,
Like sprinkles on a cake.
It tops off its beauty.
The roar of the engines
Doesn't cover a child's shrill,
As the icy air chills me.

My space is rationed.
I insert my earplugs,
Plunging into my own world
With Pink Floyd narrating it.
I am in a place between realms
Where I can find a universe.
Here planetary poetry exists—
Above the clouds.

VACATION GONE

The island is behind me,
As the plane carries me back to the mainland.
Seated and belted I travel in limbo.
Water and cookies are handed to me.
The person who'd relaxed by the ocean—gone.
Now the person with responsibilities emerges.
Plans and lists are made as I'm carried back to my life.
Gone are the mornings of a carefree breakfast
Gone are the views of waves crashing on the shore
Gone are the lazy morning snorkels
Gone are what awaits under the waves
Gone is asking, "What do you want to do today?"
Gone is the answer, "Relax."
Gone is the lunch eaten on the lanai
Gone is dinner overlooking the sunset
Gone is the flock of parrots filling the skies
Gone is sleeping in until I'm ready to get up.
That is all behind me...
As I race forward back to my life.
The same person who left, yet changed
After spending some time on an island
One that I left behind, yet part of it left with me.

POETRY IN THE AIR

Words go on paper just like always
Written with a pen: thoughts and feelings.
But it comes from a different place,
Above the landscape where the air is thin.
Where no birds dare to fly.
The only people I will meet...
Are seated around me.
Travelers with the same destination.
Here the words come to me differently,
Because I'm surrounded by beings.
Music has promised me privacy with headphones.
Out my window floats water-filled clouds,
While inside it rains with human existence.
So, unlike my solitude of writing at home,
Airborne is an unaware collective effort,
All becoming a part of poetry in the air.

KEEP

Our plane takes us to where we want to go.
Perched in our seat, strapped and plugged in.
We sit in a journey offered drinks and snacks,
With a quick trip to the bathroom while waiting.
Although the plane takes us to the next destination
It is not without a bit of turbulence...
Just like in life we keep going forward.

WAITING

Our lives are defined more clearly
As we're seated in a plane in coach.
Each light bump pushes us into each other
Reminding us of our existence in this body.
Lines form for human functions in narrow aisles.
We squeeze our way through, only barest needs met
It's a pleasure standing tall and stretching.
Since our legroom's limited by our possessions
They've carefully niched us into our allotted space
With forms of quiet entertainment or sleep.
Just passing some time in limbo's breath.
We eagerly await the next event in life
Because we're squeezed into this moment
Each a moving part of a separate unit, waiting.

RUSH

Rush to the airport—sweat dripping.
What did you forget?
The rental was returned,
Boarding pass printed,
The luggage checked in.
Your heart races through security
You're pulled aside with your carry-on.
Garments awkwardly scattered on the table.
Found...
A small pocketknife placed in the wrong bag.
It's quickly disposed of and you forge ahead.
After purchasing water, you locate your gate.
Finally, it is time to board the plane, so you line up.
Slowly moving in the lengthy line...
Finally make your way to your seat.
Here you rush to find a space above you,
To place your loved one's treasures and yours...
Only after some minor rearranging.
Your rush now done. You relax—until the exodus.

BONUS POETRY

THE OLD WOMAN

The old woman follows the night.
Quietly submerged in amethyst...
As her robes stroke the hard ground.
The stars are her guide.

The changing moon is her light
As her eyes pierce the darkness.
Her feet are safely wrapped in leather
She keeps moving forward.

Her walking stick is strong and sturdy
She follows the untouched path
Through the hushed frozen forest
She maneuvers the terrain.

She might trip or fall over the obstacles
But that doesn't stop her
She always gets back up
Because her destination awaits.

She knows the bearded old man
Is making the same journey
In another time...
In another place.

In that moment when they meet
They will both be home.
But, the old woman's journey
Has only just begun.

So, without stopping or resting
She keeps walking...
Bravely into the darkness
Toward the promised bliss.

THE BEARDED OLD MAN (*No Fairy Tale*)

The bearded old man
Walks across the quiet desert,
His hooded white robe
Protecting and sheltering him
From the burning sky.
His feet are silent against the sand.
He walks day and night,
Going to a place that he knows exists.
He beckons strangers to join him
As he keeps walking toward...
That place he calls home.

SOME READERS' FAVORITES FROM
No Fairy Tale

ANOTHER WORLD

Deep under the sea
Is another place,
Not just for fish
Or humans to explore.
It's their world,
Unseen by mortal eyes.
They know it isn't safe
To show themselves just yet.
They welcome back
Another one
Who had been lost
From their fold.
They are safe,
And they wait
For their time
To come forth.
Until then they watch,
Wait, and swim
With the dolphins,
Hiding in plain sight.

OCEAN

If I close my eyes, I can picture the ocean.
I can hear the sounds of it washing upon the shores.
Breathing in, I can almost taste the salt air I crave,
And feel the sun and wind, as the sand caresses my bare feet
As I turn my attention to the funny little birds running,
They are trying to eat before the next wave crashes in.
A plane flies by low, back and forth over the shore,
Silently searching for what I don't know.
I walk toward the water away from the plane's chaotic search.
The sand is warm and dry on my toes, when a cold wave hits.
It takes my breath away, then the wave retreats.
Empty crab shells are scattered from quick bird meals.
I spot an iridescent blue abalone and a sculpted gray clam
    shell.
Even the food is beautiful here.
I walk on in deep peace that I can only feel at the ocean.
My family chases the waves with squeals and glee.
I smile.
Alone, I meditate in silent breaths, open to the wonder.
Satisfied, I rejoin my clan renewed and centered.
We write our names in the wet sand,
Finish short-lived castles and search the tide pools,
With a hopeful glance thrown to spot a dolphin or whale.
Then we settle down for a sandy snack that tastes better at the
    seashore.
We fill our bodies' hunger and the ocean fills our souls' appetite.
Yes, I can see all of this when I close my eyes,
Because I've done it so many times—yet never enough.

TREES

You stand together
In a tall group,
Still, silent, and strong.
You stretch to the heavens
Yet pull life from the earth.
You drink from the cool rains,
You bask in the warm sun,
You bend with the heavy winds,
You sleep in the icy snow,
Your green branches heavy with it.
You grant shade,
Provide homes,
Provide food,
Provide air.
You never ask for anything in return.
All you need is supplied
By the nature encompassing you.
You protect all who come to you,
Even your predators:
Man, drought, insects, and fire.
The bears, the birds, the squirrels,
Yes, even humans you comfort—no judgment.
You are strong yet gentle.
You watch things that
Never change.

You observe things that
Always change,
Breathing the same air,
Drinking the same water.
Your survival depends on the masses.
You aren't just
A solitary tree
In a forest,
But the whole forest
In perfection.

MEADOW

The sun bears down on me and warms my cold skin.
My dress is antiquated in magnificence,
And my hair frames me like a golden halo.
My bare feet frolic in joy on the soft, green turf.
It's plusher than any putting green or manmade carpet.
The fragrant scents of pines and wild roses.
Crisp, pure water rushing down the falls,
Into the clear pond below awaken my senses.
The wind rustles the trees and the birds sing in flight.
I offer my arms above my head,
As a bliss-filled greeting to my private meadow.
Secluded in the lush forest I embrace freedom,
Dancing with abandon, I'm free and light.
Happy and carefree—rapture fills every cell
In my body. In my leaps and bounds
I twirl, sing, and laugh as the water beckons me
I slip into the welcoming pool of water.
Spinning and kicking, my happiness complete now.
Finally I leave the water behind,
As I lie on the sweet grass and absorb the sun's warmth.
Everything is perfect in my created sanctuary.
A place where pain, suffering, anxiety, grief, and illness
Have never been allowed and sadness is yet unseen.
A place to sit and just be.
A rainbow caresses my hand and it careens my soul
I've found pure happiness. I am safe. I am home.

SENSES

The glow of your face
That soothed my eyes is gone.
The aroma of your skin is lost
Like a rose's scent in the icy dawn.
The taste of your essence
Left my lips too soon,
The warmth of your body, gone, leaving
Our bed an empty cocoon.
My senses rebel against your absence
While my soul reaches out, finds you,
And desperately hangs on until
You fill my senses again, as only you can do.

HELLO

Hello, it's me.
Been so long
Since we've talked.
How are things?
Busy? Me too!
No time to meet this week.
Next week?
No, Monday isn't good for me.
I'll call you back,
Or...sure, you can call me.
Evenings are better
Unless I'm not here.
What? The kids? They're fine.
I'd thought they'd
Be easier as they got older.
But yours, too?
No wonder we're tired
So busy
Have no time.
Oh, I should go.
There's one to pick up soon.
We'll get together.
Thanks for the call, but...
Yeah, we always used to be together.
Now we hardly even talk on the phone.

How things have changed
For us;
But not our kids.
Soon, but not now.
What will we do with all that free time?
What? You are caring for your aging parents, too?
I just started last year, shopping and cleaning.
Yes, when we get some free time, we will.
Got to go. You too, bye.
Another part of life slowly fades away

FINGERS OF THE SEA

The weightless world of the beach engulfs me
As the long, extended fingers of the sea
Gently
Stroke me—welcome me,
Enticing with its salty breath,
Satisfying my deep, hidden hunger.
Slowly
The fingers curl back
An invitation,
Beckoning toward the heart of the sea.
Beneath my gaze on the cold, wet world
Its subjects are sent out to tempt,
Screeching and scurrying
Above and below me,
All in a frenzied orchestrated rhythm.
The sea's haunting song
Urgently
Seduces my soul.
All of my resistance floats away
Like the curling waves,
As I blissfully clutch
The fingers of the sea.

SUNSET

They sat entwined,
Bodies with no boundaries,
A moment of perfection
On a balcony above a pool
Filled with lotion-lathered kids
Beyond where waves meet sand
And the sea carries small offerings
That hand-holding couples
Bow down to harvest.
The sinking sun's colors
Bathed everything
In red, orange, and yellow.
The glow was broken only
By lingering shadows of
A coconut tree.
The couple smiled and kissed
In their own secluded realm,
Illuminated by the sunset.

OCEAN SONG

You are perched high
Above the sea
Among the rocky cliffs,
Hair flowing in the breeze
As you gently play your guitar.

Your clothes, like the Renaissance,
Are from a time in the past.
Your music hauntingly sweet
As the winds carry it away
To be heard by exotic ears.

The songs are waiting for you
To find them,
Deeply buried
Within the pounding waters
In a rhythmic beat.

The ocean
Plays music on its shore.
These songs
Anticipate your arrival.
And so do I. I wait.

Author's Note

Nature inspires my writing. The change of the seasons has always invoked different emotions: growth, rest, abundance, scarcity, peace, and fear—just like the seasons in my own life. I wrote these poems in a plane, in my front yard, on a beach, in a car, on a motorcycle, in a forest, or in various places in my house. The most challenging place to write was sitting on the back of my husband's Harley while maneuvering through the roads and wind. I'm proud to say I never lost a pen or piece of paper doing so. In writing the paranormal books *The Button* and *This Second Chance* they inspired me to write poetry on the topics of abuse and evil. *No Fairy Tale* was a different type of memoir that included poetry. I decided to add some of the favorites mentioned in reviews here and a couple of family's favorites, too. This rounded off my first poetry collection.

Before I go, I must thank my family for being so supportive of me writing poetry—and books. Some of the photographs you see were possible thanks to me yelling, *Stop I have to take a picture of that!* to my most patient husband. My animals were always there as my muses, especially when I wrote outdoors. And thanks to *Artful Editor* for making this readable! My biggest thanks goes to you for reading this! If you enjoyed it, please consider leaving a short review. It's the best gift you can give an author.

About the Author

 D.L. Finn is an independent California local who encourages everyone to embrace their inner child. She was born and raised in the foggy Bay Area, but in 1990 relocated with her husband, kids, dogs, and cats to the Sierra foothills in Nevada City, CA. She immersed herself in reading all types of books, but especially loved romance, horror, and fantasy. She always treasured creating her own reality on paper. Finally, being surrounded by towering pines, oaks, and cedars, her creativity was nurtured until it bloomed. Her creations vary from children's books, young adult fantasy, and adult paranormal romance to an autobiography with poetry. She continues on her adventures with an open invitation for her readers to join her.

www.ingramcontent.com/pod-product-compliance
Lightning Source LLC
Chambersburg PA
CBHW070732020526
44118CB00035B/1184